JUST WHEN YOU THOUGHT
YOU'D HEARD THEM ALL!

An irresistible collection of side-splitting gags
and guffaws that will leave you lame with laughter!

HAVE YOU HEARD ABOUT THE POL-
ISH GODFATHER?

HE'LL MAKE YOU AN OFFER YOU
CAN'T UNDERSTAND.

WACKY! WONDERFUL! BOISTEROUS!
BAWDY!

THE ABSOLUTELY LAST
OFFICIAL POLISH JOKE BOOK

Bantam Books by Larry Wilde
Ask your bookseller for the books you have missed

The *Last* Official Smart Kids Joke Book
The *Absolutely Last* Official Polish Joke Book
The *Last* Official Irish Joke Book
The *Last* Official Sex Maniacs Joke Book
The Larry Wilde Book of Limericks
The Official Lawyers Joke Book
The Official Doctors Joke Book
The *Last* Official Jewish Joke Book

THE Absolutely Last OFFICIAL POLISH JOKE BOOK

LARRY WILDE

Illustrations by Ron Wing

BANTAM BOOKS

TORONTO • NEW YORK • LONDON • SYDNEY • AUCKLAND

THE ABSOLUTELY LAST OFFICIAL POLISH JOKE BOOK
A Bantam Book / August 1983

All rights reserved.
Copyright © 1983 by Larry Wilde.
Cover art copyright © 1983 by Ron Wing.
This book may not be reproduced in whole or in part, by
mimeograph or any other means, without permission.
For information address: Bantam Books, Inc.

ISBN 0-553-20929-9

Published simultaneously in the United States and Canada

Bantam Books are published by Bantam Books, Inc. Its trademark, consisting of the words "Bantam Books" and the portrayal of a rooster, is Registered in U.S. Patent and Trademark Office and in other countries. Marca Registrada. Bantam Books, Inc., 666 Fifth Avenue, New York, New York 10103.

PRINTED IN THE UNITED STATES OF AMERICA

O   0 9 8 7 6 5 4 3 2

*To John Ziccardi—
a lovable Italian
with Irish spirit,
Jewish salesmanship,
and a passion for telling
Polish jokes.*

Contents

Introduction

You are now holding in your hands an extremely unusual object. It is an unprecedented, astonishing, extraordinary phenomenon. *"But,"* you say, *"it's only another book of Polish jokes. What's the big deal?"*

Just this: Throughout America, ethnic humor, in general, is at the peak of its popularity, and Polish jokes, in particular, are more prevalent than ever.

Over the years, Mexican, black, Italian, Irish, and Jewish jokes have flourished and continued to proliferate in great abundance. Jokes about these major minorities have been traded over such a long period of time that they have become part and parcel of American humor. In fact, around Southern California, wags lump together several ethnic groups when relating this classic:

Why is Sunday morning the best time to be on a Los Angeles freeway?

The Catholics are in church.

The Protestants are still asleep.

The Jews are in Palm Springs.

The Indians are restricted to the reservation.

The Chinese are stuffing fortune cookies.

The Blacks are in jail.

And the Mexicans can't get their cars started.

In spite of the high priority for telling many types of yarns with ethnic overtones, the Polish joke craze continues unabated. No other gag fad—elephant jokes, sick jokes, shaggy dog jokes, good news/bad news jokes, etc.—has lasted as long or evoked as much controversy.

How come?

The humor of ridicule evokes belly laughs. Not smiles or chuckles or titters but genuine, real, from-the-gut guffaws. (Only material of a sexual nature garners greater audience reaction.)

For whatever psychological reasons, it seems to be part of human nature for most people to put down others in such a way that it makes them feel superior. The most powerful thrust in comedy is mockery. In ethnic humor, particular traits of a specific group are exaggerated and stretched for comedy purposes.

There are some overly sensitive Poles who feel these sidesplitters are derisive and demeaning. It is their belief that these rapierlike jests poke fun at an entire minority. Yet there are millions of Polish Americans who vehemently disagree with this point of view.

During the promotion of three previous Polish joke books throughout the United States, I talked with hundreds of people who said, "I'm Polish, and I think it's important to have a sense of humor. I love Polish jokes."

Or, "I'm married to a Pole, and we have lots of fun with Polish jokes. You can't take them seriously."

What it boils down to is one's ability to "take a joke." How good a sense of humor do you have? Are you easily offended by personal comments? Are you secure enough to handle a jibe—any kind of jest—whether it's about your weight, nose, baldness, mother-in-law, wife, girlfriend, or your ethnic background?

The truly amazing aspect of the current humor phenomenon is that what we refer to as "Polish" jokes are in reality not even Polish. Quips that come out of Poland are a completely different brand of humor. They are based on the political and economic climate of that country.

For example, since meat has been rationed in Poland and the lines outside stores are endless, the following joke is making the rounds:

"Where are you headed?" one Pole asks another.

"To Cracow to get some meat."

"But there's no meat in Cracow. The only meat is in Warsaw."

"I know, but the line starts in Cracow."

Although humor in Poland encompasses every complexity of the human condition, one subject that has the sharpest edge is politics. Combine that with a bit of erotica and you have the perfect combination for a potential belly laugh:

A local party secretary asked Comrade Komalski why he doesn't come for ideological instruction every Wednesday and Saturday evening. "I don't need it," replied Kamolski.

"You do. And I prove it. Who was Karl Marx?"

"I don't know."

"Who was Vladimir Ilyich Lenin?"

"I don't know," said Kamolski.

"There, I told you," barked the party boss.

"But wait," said Kamolski. "You ask me about all those people, now let me ask you: Who is Jozef Olecki?"

"I have no idea," answered the secretary.

"See?" said Kamolski. "But I know that one. While you're at ideo-logical instruction every Wednesday and Saturday night, Jozef Olecki is screwing your wife."

There is still another fascinating slant to the Polish joke rage. The japes are interchangeable. If you live around San Francisco, the very same gags are called *Portuguese*. In South Dakota, they're *Norwegian*. All over Canada, they are told as *Newfie* jokes (after the people who reside in Newfoundland). And guess what? In Texas, these same inane, sarcastic, moronic, insidi-ous slurs are known as *Aggie* jokes (told about students at Texas Agricultural and Mining University).

The big question is How do we stop this avalanche of disrespectful and disparag-ing wit? How can you prevent people from passing on to each other that which titillates, amuses, and entertains?

The end is not in sight, as witnessed by the following story originating on the East Coast:

Lowandowski went to a Long Is-land night club and listened to a ven-triloquist tell one Polish joke after another. Finally, he'd had enough. The

5

Pole got to his feet and shouted, "I'm fed up with these Polish jokes. What makes you think we are all that stupid?"

"Please, mister," said the ventriloquist. "These are only jokes, and I've never met a Pole yet who didn't have a sense of humor."

"I not talkin' to you," raged the Polack. "I be talkin' to that little fella on your knee."

Ribbing, razzing, and roasting in the United States is as commonplace as hamburgers and hot dogs. The wisecrack is our traditional form of the jest. No other country in the world can make that boast. No other country has the freedom of expression, security, or inclination to laugh at itself.

Poking fun, twitting, teasing, and hazing are at the very core of our humor folklore. If you outlaw these comedic forms, you take away the guts, the very essence, of the American sense of humor.

Then what do we do?

Laugh, my friends, laugh. As that British fella from Stratford-on-Avon once said, "Laugh and the world laughs with you, cry and you appear on *Real People*."

LARRY WILDE

Hodgepodgeski

What do you call a Polack who practices birth control.
A humanitarian.

* * *

Why is the average age of a Polish soldier fifty-seven?
They get them right out of high school.

* * *

* * *

Majeski went into a hardware store and bought two dozen mothballs. The next day he went back and asked for another twenty-four.

"But you bought two dozen only yesterday," observed the owner.

"I know," said the Polack, "but those moths are very hard to hit."

* * *

Kowecki went to the movie house, bought his ticket, and then went in to see the film. In a minute, he reappeared at the box office and bought another ticket. A few minutes later, he came back and asked for another ticket.

"What's the idea?" questioned the cashier. "I've already sold you two tickets."

"I know," said the Polack, "but every time I try to get in, some dummy keeps tearing them up."

* * *

POLISH FILM

Escape to Alcatraz

* * *

Murphy: Hey, Krulka, why do you pick your nose with your finger?

Krulka: Because my tongue ain't long enough.

* * *

Did you hear about the Polack who couldn't tell the difference between Vaseline and putty?

His windowpane fell out.

Then there was a Polack who had just learned to count to twenty-one when he was arrested for indecent exposure.

* * *

A man in a hospital accidentally had a bowel movement in his bed. He didn't want the nurses to find it, so he gathered up the sheet and threw it out the window. It landed on Jursykowski as he was walking by.

The Polack disentangled himself from the sheet but got the mess all over himself. Shaken, he walked into a bar and ordered a beer. "Boy, you stink," said the bartender.

"You would, too," replied the Polack, "if you beat the doo-doo out of a ghost who flew out of a third-story window."

* * *

POLISH PARTY GAME

Pin the Horns on the Donkey

* * *

Milewkawicz and Filipowski went to Cleveland on vacation, got drunk, and ended up at a party in the house of someone they didn't know. They woke the next morning in their hotel room with heavy hangovers.

"That party last night sure was great," said Milewkawicz.

"Yeah," said Filipowski, "but I don't believe we thanked the hosts. Let's go back and tell them."

"Okay," said Milewkawicz, "but all I remember is that the house had a gold commode."

They knocked on practically every door in the neighborhood and asked what color commode they had. Finally, they came to the last house. "Do you have a gold commode?" asked Milewkawicz.

The woman who answered the door yelled back to her husband, "Harry! we finally found the guy who crapped in the tuba!"

* * *

* * *

Did you hear about the two Polacks who drowned trying to dig a cellar in their houseboat?

Then there was the Polack who bought $3,000 worth of tires for his house because he wanted white walls.

* * *

Halicki sent his son to a university; after a while, the boy was awarded his B.A. On graduation, he received the following telegram from his father:
"Congratulations on your B.A. Now for the other twenty-four letters and this time try to get them in the right order."

* * *

A Polish newspaper once printed the following notice on its front page:
"Today we present our Crossword Contest, first prize $1,000. But those of you who want to do it just for fun and don't want to wait until next week for the answers, you can find the solution on the back page."

* * *

Bettyann Kevles, the nifty novelist, heard this newy at a Cal Poly teachers' luncheon.

Tiffingham, Duval, and Linkowski were shipwrecked and floating on a raft in the middle of the Atlantic. The three men had been on the water for several weeks without food or water and were close to death. Suddenly, they spotted a floating bottle. The Frenchman opened it, and out popped a genie. "Gentlemen," he said, "you have freed me from my prison, and as a reward I will grant three wishes between you."

"Oh," said Duval, "I wish I was back in Paris."

The genie snapped his fingers, and the Frenchman disappeared. "I, sir," said the Englishman, "wish I were in London."

Again, the genie snapped his fingers, and Tiffingham was gone. "What would you like?" asked the genie of Linkowski.

"Gee," said the Polack, "I miss those guys. I wish they were back here!"

"The goldfish must be very happy today."

"What makes you say that?"

"Well, just look at it. It's wagging its tail."

* * *

Did you hear about the two Polacks who went ice fishing?

They caught three hundred pounds of ice and drowned trying to fry it.

And then there was the Polack who was invited to play in a floating crap game, so he showed up in a bathing suit and inner tube.

* * *

Linkowicz admired Minnelli's alligator shoes. "How much they be?" he asked.

"They cost ninety-five dollars," replied the Italian.

The Pole thought that was too much to pay for a pair of shoes, so he went to the swamp and hunted for an alligator.

Linkowicz found a gigantic alligator, jumped in, wrestled it, and finally pulled it from the water. "Dammit, just my luck," moaned the Polack. "This alligator is barefooted!"

* * *

POLISH NEWSPAPER ADVERTISEMENT

For Sale:
All kinds of homemade antiques.

* * *

Why don't doctors circumcise Polacks anymore?
They discovered they were throwing away the best part.

* * *

Jenlinseika was being examined by his doctor. "If you really are sincere about losing weight," advised the doctor, "then I want you to take a daily walk on an empty stomach.
"Okay," said the Polack. "But whose?"

* * *

NEWS ITEM

Witold Kowalczyk was admitted to the city hospital last night with severe burns after dunking for French fries at a Halloween party.

* * *

*   *   *

After his examination, Bratkowski sat at the doctor's desk.

"Take these pills two days running, then skip a day," said the M.D. "Follow this routine for two weeks, then report back to me."

At the end of one week, Bratkowski went back to the doctor. "I'm tired," he complained. "That skipping wore me out."

*   *   *

"I tell you, that Wlasowica is getting to be a real snob."

"Why you say that?"

"He's got ashtrays in his house with no advertising on them!"

*   *   *

MacManus the policeman was having dinner with his wife. "Anything interesting happen today?" she asked her husband.

"Yeah. We arrested a Polack when he made an obscene phone call and reversed the charges."

*   *   *

*   *   *

Did you hear about the Polish grandmother who went on the pill?

She didn't want to have any more grandchildren.

*   *   *

Stanley took Gloria out driving in the country. He parked the car in a lover's lane but just sat there. Gloria decided to make the first move.

She said, "Stanley, would you like to see where I had my operation?"

"No, I hate hospitals," said the Polack.

*   *   *

Doctor Barnes was walking through the Cleveland General Hospital ward one morning. Suddenly, he noticed a man in the corner bed who kept scratching his elbow.

The doctor said to the head nurse, "What's wrong with him?"

"He has hemorrhoids," she replied.

"Then why is he scratching his elbow?"

"He's a Polack, and he doesn't know his ass from his elbow," said the nurse.

*   *   *

Beverly Blitzer, the Hancock Park chic boutique entrepreneur, collapses customers with this bon mot:

Lomanecki walked into a saloon with a front door under his arm.

"Why are you carrying that door?" asked the barman.

"Well," said the Polack, "last night I lost the key, so in case anybody finds it and breaks into my house, I'm carrying the door around."

"But what happens if you lose the door?"

"That's okay," said Lomanecki. "I left the window open."

19

Did you hear about the Polack who died of six hundred stab wounds in the forehead?

He was trying to teach himself to eat with a fork.

And then, of course, there was the Polack who tried to tunnel his way out of a prison ship.

* * *

Why are there only twenty hours in a Polish day?

Have you ever seen a Polack with twenty-four fingers and toes?

* * *

Jackowski walked up to an airport ticket counter and asked, ''When be the next plane to Buffalo?''

''At three-thirty this afternoon,'' replied the clerk. ''But it's a local flight with stop-overs in Pittsburgh and New York. The whole flight will take about four hours.''

''That be too long,'' said Jackowski.

''The best I can do on a direct flight is the day after tomorrow,'' said the clerk.

''Okay, I wait for that one,'' said the Polack.

* * *

*   *   *

How do you recognize an airplane designed by a Polack?
It has outside toilets.

*   *   *

What do you call the index finger on a Polack's left hand?
A handkerchief.

*   *   *

Why can't Polacks lie on the beach?
Cats will bury them.

*   *   *

"I finally got a date with Rosemary last night."
"Yeah? How you make out?"
"She wanted to play post office, but we didn't play. She wasn't there when I got back from the drugstore with the stamps."

*   *   *

Why do flies have wings?
So they can beat the Polacks to the garbage cans.

*   *   *

Have you heard about the Polack who spent three hours in a car wash?

He thought it was raining too hard to drive.

*　*　*

Domanski had dinner at his friend Pieracki's house. Both men ate and drank into the late hours. It was pitch black out when Domanski started for home, so his host provided him with a flashlight.

About two hours later, there was a loud knock on Pieracki's door. "Who is it?" he shouted from inside.

"It only be me," said Domanski. "I came back to return your flashlight. I be able to find my way home without it."

*　*　*

How do you recognize a roll of Polish toilet paper?

Look for the instructions printed on each sheet.

*　*　*

What is the most popular Polish song? "Shoo, Fly, Don't Bother Me."

*　*　*

* * *

Did you hear about the Polack who designed the coolest submarine? It has a screen door.

Don't knock it. It keeps the fish out.

Then there was the Polack who thought Cheerios were doughnut seeds.

* * *

How can we be sure that Santa Claus is a Polack?

There are two doors in the average house and eight windows, but he comes down the chimney.

* * *

Gabrzyszwski got on a double-decker bus for the first time in Los Angeles. After bothering a passenger for several minutes, he took the passenger's advice and went up on the deck.

Soon he came down again, and the passenger asked, ''Why didn't you stay up on the other deck?''

''You think I'm crazy?'' said the Polack. ''There be no driver up there.''

* * *

Kopacki and his friend Cinelli were sitting near the ocean at Revere Beach. Suddenly, a sensationally stacked girl strolled by and winked at Kopacki. He turned to his pal and said, "What should I do?"

"Wink back," said the Italian.

He did.

Then the girl winked and also smiled at Kopacki. He asked his friend what he should do.

"Wink and smile back at her," advised Cinelli.

He did.

Then the girl removed the top of her bikini and dropped the bottom string. "Wow," said Kopacki, "what do I do now?"

"Show her your nuts," said his buddy.

The Polack put his thumbs in his ears, waved, stuck out his tongue, and howled "Bla-Bla-Bla-Bla!"

Polacheck took his friend Lipska driving in the mountains. After a while, Lipska said, "Every time you race around one of those sharp curves, I get scared!"

"Then why don't you do what I do?" said Polacheck. "Close your eyes."

* * *

POLISH CAR POOL

They meet at work.

* * *

What is the national fruit of Poland?
Monkey-wrench nuts.

* * *

A bunch of the boys at the Silver Dollar Saloon decided to play a dirty trick on the Polish cowboy. While he was getting drunk, they turned his horse around and put the saddle on backward.

Next morning, his wife shouted at him, "Get up! You gotta get out on the trail."

"I'm so tired, Marianna. Somebody cut my horses' head off, and I had to lead him home with my finger in his windpipe."

* * *

What is a wrench?
That's where Polish cowboys lived.

* * *

Zajaczkowsky got off the bus in a small Texas town for a rest stop. He spotted a cowboy and said, "What that long rope for?"

"That's for catching cows," replied the Texan.

"No kidding," said the Polack. "What you use for bait?"

* * *

Banacek had never been outside Hamtramck and decided to hitchhike to California.

One morning, he approached a rancher in Montana and said, "Hey, mista, why you cows have no horns?"

"Because," answered the rancher, "those are horses."

* * *

How do you recognize a Polack staying in a fancy hotel?

He's the one trying to slam the revolving door.

* * *

* * *

Did you hear about the Polish skier with the frostbitten fanny?

He couldn't figure how to get his pants over the skis.

Then there was the Polack who thought Taco Bell was a Mexican phone company.

* * *

NEWS ITEM

We regret to announce the death of Monk Razdick, the leading Polish water polo player, who was drowned when he fell off his pony.

* * *

Janczik wandered around backstage between the acts of a musical revue. He started to enter a room clearly marked:

CHORUS GIRLS DRESSING ROOM.
POSITIVELY NO ADMITTANCE.

The stage manager caught him by the arm. "Can't you read?" he hollered, pointing at the sign.

"Who's smoking?" demanded Janczik.

* * *

28

Casmir the con man went to New York, but he didn't have much luck. The first man to whom he tried to sell the Brooklyn Bridge turned out to be the owner, and the Polack had to pay him $100 so he wouldn't tell the cops.

* * *

Kowalski and Shaunessy were having a philosophical discussion on dairy products.

"Why the devil is cream so much more expensive than milk?" asked the Irishman.

"Well," explained the Polack, "cream is dearer because they find it harder to make the cows sit on the smaller bottles."

* * *

Kulac sat in the optometrist's examination room having his eyes tested.

"Read the bottom line," said the optician.

"S-K-R-O-W-Z-I-E-W-I-C-Z. . . . Hey, I know that guy!"

* * *

To keep down the rising birth rate among animals, the Warsaw Zoo has shot all the storks.

* * *

A large Midwestern zoo advertised their lions, Brutus and Rommel, as the two most vicious in the world. There was no doubt about Brutus, the smaller one, for if even a paper bag came within reach, he would pounce on it and rip it to shreds.

However, Rommel, the larger lion, did nothing but lie against some rocks, licking between his hind legs.

A tourist asked the zoo keeper why Rommel was supposed to be so savage.

"I know he's just lying there licking his sensitive areas," explained the zoo keeper, "but Rommel's more ferocious than Brutus. In fact, not twenty minutes ago, he ate a Polack that fell into the cage!"

"Then why is he licking himself like that?"

"Oh," said the keeper, "He's trying to get the taste out of his mouth!"

* * *

THE POLISH NATIONAL ANTHEM

Sing Something Simple

* * *

Novack, a steelworker, went to an optometrist for an examination. "Cup your hand and put it over your right eye."

The steelworker cupped his left hand and placed it on his forehead.

"No," said the optometrist, "cup your hand and cover your eye."

Novak cupped his right hand and covered his forehead.

The optometrist took a large paper bag and placed it over the steelworker's head. Then he cut out a hole in the bag over his left eye. Suddenly, tears formed in Novack's eye. The optometrist immediately cut a hole in the bag over his right eye. Again, tears formed in Novack's eyes.

"For God's sake," shouted the doctor, "why are you crying."

"Oh," sobbed the Polack, "I was really hoping I'd get wire rims."

*   *   *

Boyskis

How does a Polish boy scout start a fire?

By rubbing two matches together.

* * *

"I wonder why my shaving brush is so stiff."

"Dunno, dad. It was all right yesterday when I painted the canary's cage with it."

* * *

What do you call a Polack with half a brain?

Gifted!

* * *

What do you call a Polack with a degree?

A liar!

Did you hear about the Polack who lost a contact lens when the putty fell out of his eye?

Or the Polack who went looking for a gas leak with a safety match?

Then there was the Polish mugger who wore white bowling shoes so he wouldn't leave footprints in the snow.

* * *

Marino and Sawicki were having a beer.
"I saw you out on the town last night," said the Italian. "How'd you make out?"
"Great," replied Sawicki. "I met this lady taxi driver—and what a terrific time we had!"
"A lady taxi-driver?" asked Marino. "How could you tell?"
"Easy," said the other Polack, "All night long she kept going out on calls."

* * *

"Peter Rezlitski, I arrest you for breaking into the Metropolitan Museum."
"Hey, officer, how you catch me so quick?"
"You shouldn't've signed the visitor's book."

Kuczynski was not a TV fan. He liked outdoor sports. But once a week he always settled in front of the set to see the same opening shots of one particular sitcom. On the screen, a girl was taking off her clothes to swim in a nearby lake. Just as she was about to remove the last garment, a train flashed past in the foreground and blotted her from view.

"Damn!" the Polack said to himself. "That train be on time again!"

* * *

What is a Polack's idea of ultimate comfort?

A fur-lined condom.

* * *

POLISH SPORT

Water-skiing through a car wash

* * *

Thieves broke into the library of Professor Pavlik and stole two of his most valued books. "The thing that upsets me the most," said the Polish professor, "is that I hadn't finished coloring in one of them."

* * *

Dobrienski walked into a saloon and gave an order to the bartender. "Give me five martinis and line them all up on the bar!"

"Sure," said the barkeep. "What's the occasion?"

"I just got my first blow job!"

"That's great? Let me add one to it and make it six!"

"Ah, hell," said the Polack. "If five don't get the taste out, nothing will!"

* * *

Passenger: Hey, watch out, he's driving right at you!

Kachowski: Well, two can play at that game, you know. Hold tight.

* * *

Did you hear about the nearsighted Polack who dropped his cigar inside a dog kennel?

He picked up and lit fifteen of them before he discovered the right one.

Then there was the Polack who returned a half-used bag of cat litter to the pet shop. He complained that no matter how he served up the stuff, his cat just wouldn't eat it.

* * *

How can you tell the Polack at the Off-Track Betting parlor?

He's the one with the binoculars.

* * *

Callahan had been drinking all day in a saloon. Late in the day, he came out of the men's room and said to the bartender, "Y-y-ou're n-not gonna believe this, but there's a nigger in there with a white pecker!"

"Nah," said the bartender. "he's just a Polack coal miner that goes home for lunch."

* * *

Then there were the two Polacks who played pool every night and never pocketed a ball—till somebody suggested they take the wooden frame away.

* * *

"Hey, Bijeck, I've taken up tennis."

"Really. What position do you play?"

* * *

Why are the lights on a Polish air strip always so dim?

They point downward.

Bobbie Ross, the nimble-fingered Los Angeles hair stylist, snickers over this spirit lifter:

A cowboy on a Montana dude ranch watched Drumsticki trying to saddle a horse.

"Pardon me," he said politely, "but you're puttin' the saddle on backwards."

"What make you so sure?" asked the Polack. "How you know what direction I be goin'?"

Have you heard about the Polack's obscene phone call?

He said, "You've a lovely voice and sound very sexy but don't keep telling me the time."

* * *

"Does Lewonski know anything about sports?"

"You kiddin'? He thinks shuttlecock and golf balls are ailments like tennis elbow and athlete's foot."

* * *

Santucci took his budy Koslow hunting.

"If I miss the bird with the first shot," said the Italian, "I always hit it with my second."

"Well," said the Polack, "to save cartridges, why not fire the second shot first?"

* * *

Cusick asked his girl's father for her hand in marriage. "The thing is," said the parent, "do you think you can make Sheila happy?"

"By Jesus," said the Polack, "you should've seen her last night at the motel."

WARSAW TV SPORTS ANNOUNCER

"The Polish Round-The-World Yacht Race has just been announced: If it rains, it'll be held indoors."

"In yesterday's Olympic track tryouts, the Polish sprinter was lapped in the one-hundred-yard race."

* * *

Stefanski came into the dorm from his morning classes, flopped down on his bed, and said to his roommate Bourke, "I'm bushed. I'm going to sleep a while, but I have a two P.M. class, so I can't sleep very long."

Just before falling asleep, Stefanski said to Bourke, "Are you going to be here for a while?"

"Yeah," said his roommate.

"Good," said the Polack. "I'll let you know if I want you to wake me up!"

* * *

What do you call a Polish brain surgeon. A chiropodist.

* * *

Nowicki had a bad breath problem and went to the doctor. The physician gave him a series of tests and told him to come back the following day for his diagnosis.

When he returned, the doctor said, "You have to do one of two things—either quit scratching your ass or quit biting your fingernails."

* * *

The Detroit culinary workers are still talking about it: a Polack walked into a restaurant, sat down at a table, called the waiter over, and said, "I be in a big hell of a hurry. Just bring me bill!"

* * *

What are the rules of the famous Polish guessing game?

One player leaves the room, and the others have to guess which one of them has left.

* * *

Morrie Feldman, the super Santa Rosa podiatrist, gets screams from patients with this playful pearl:

Glowacki was driving through apple country in northern California. He stopped

42

at an orchard and asked the owner, "How much be the apples?"

"All you can pick for one dollar," said the farmer.

"Okay," said the Polack, "I'll take two dollars' worth."

* * *

Did you hear about the Polack who tried to stand on his hands?

He broke both of them when he stepped on them.

Then there was the lazy Polack who had a hernia transplant so he wouldn't have to lift anything heavy.

* * *

Did you read about the Polack who didn't know how to write the number 11?

He didn't know which 1 came first.

Or the Polack who thought manhole covers were a new type of men's shorts?

Then there was the Polack who walked all the way from Pittsburgh to New York to join the start of the long-distance walking race.

* * *

OVERHEARD IN LOVER'S LANE

"Even if you have scruples, I'd still make love to you. . . . I been vaccinated."

* * *

Theatrical agent:	So, you want to go into show business doing a memory act? But you've never tried it before! Just how do you expect to remember anything?
Wodjawdzka:	Simple. I'll tie a piece of string around my little finger.

* * *

Steelworker Marciszewski hit a jackpot on the slots in Atlantic City and to celebrate took his wife and teenage son to Warsaw to visit his grandparents. On the way back, they stopped in Paris for a few days.

One evening, the boy went off by himself and met a French prostitute who took him to her hotel room. Young Marciszewski admitted he didn't know what to do but was eager to learn.

"You're supposed to get inside me." she explained.

"Okay," said the Polack, "but you'll let my folks know where I am, won't you?"

44

Radzwicki noticed a nail sticking out of his front door. So he removed the door and carried it up to the attic because that was where he kept the pliers.

* * *

How do you recognize a well-mannered Polack?

He doesn't blow his soup—he fans it with his cap.

* * *

"Where'd you go for your holidays, Wojciech?"

"Martinique."

"Where's that?"

"I not know. I flew there."

* * *

Did you hear about the Polack who put a dime in a condom?

So in case he couldn't come, he could call.

Then there was the Polish drug addict who tried to smoke pot but forgot to take the flowers out.

* * *

How do you spot a Polack in a bowling alley?

He's the one bowling overarm.

47

* * *

Bednarik and Krazewski were watching a trombone player perform. "Hey," said Bednarik, "I bet you twenty dollars he ain't swallowing that thing."

* * *

ARTICLE IN POLISH MEDICAL JOURNAL

"Are Vasectomies Hereditary?"

* * *

What's the best way to tell a Polish pirate?

He's the one with a patch over each eye!

* * *

SIGN IN FULWARSKI'S FRONT WINDOW

For Sale:
Slightly damaged car; can be seen
only after dark. Call ES 5-6789

* * *

Why is the suicide rate so low in Poland?

You can't get killed jumping out of a basement window.

* * *

The U.S. government decided to investigate the reason for the head on the tip of a man's penis. After several months of research and at a cost of $3 million, this was the conclusion:

The head on the tip of a man's love muscle is there to give pleasure to a woman.

England then decided to conduct its own research. They spent $2 million and three months later published this result:

The head of a man's penis is there to give him pleasure.

In Poland, they immediately spent $200 to research the same project. The following year, they reached this conclusion:

The head of a man's penis is there to keep the hand from slipping off.

* * *

What do they call a thirty-five-year-old Polack in the fourth grade?

A prodigy.

* * *

Louis Quinn, Tinsel Town's fun-loving funnyman, flips friends with this howler:

Mrs. Santolli walked into Jarvzelski's flower shop one morning and asked, "How much are your bunches of flowers?"

"You mean a one-dollar bunch or a two-dollar bunch? asked the owner.

"A one-dollar bunch," said the Italian woman.

"But I don't have any left," said the Polack. "I can split a two-dollar bunch for you."

"Okay."

"Fine. Do you want the petals or the stems?"

*   *   *

Innkeeper:	You can have a room overlooking Tampa bay for seventy-five dollars.
Polish Tourist:	How much is the room if I promise not to look?

*   *   *

Cirslak the cyclist went to a cycle shop and asked for a pair of bicycle clips. "Hey," said the owner, "you're pedaling with long stockings. You don't need cycle clips because you have shorts on."

"But," said the Polish racer, "I gotta have something to stop my hair from falling over my face."

*   *   *

Have you heard about the Polack who cut a hole in his umbrella?

He wanted to know when it stopped raining.

Then there was the deaf-and-dumb Polack who broke all his fingers trying to do tongue twisters.

*   *   *

The following questions and answers are from a Polish senior high school graduation exam:

Q. Name one of the Seven Wonders of the World.
A. The Eiffel Tower of Pisa.

Q. What are the four seasons?
A. Salt, mustard, vinegar, pepper.

Q. How many seconds in a year?
A. Twelve. January second, February second, March second . . .

* * *

Zabrocki was on his way to the theater to see a film of the fight between Joe Frazier and Mohammad Ali. "Where you gonna sit?" asked a chum.

"Right down front," said the Polack, "so that I can see the fight properly. I was there last night, and Joe Frazier nearly won. He be sure to beat Ali tonight!"

* * *

How do you spot a Polack in a movie theater showing a foreign film?

He's the one using his finger to read the subtitles.

* * *

Did you hear about the Polack who dropped his chewing gum in the chicken coop?

It took him a half hour to find it.

Then there was the Polack on an oil rig who, every morning, would check to see if the helicopters had laid any eggs.

And what about the Polack who paid $150 for the Unknown Soldier's autograph.

*   *   *

Waznicki couldn't read or write. So he asked his neighbor to write a letter to his father in Gadansk.

"And please," said Waznicki, "write in large letters. My father no can hear too good."

*   *   *

AD IN POLISH POP MUSIC PAPER

For Sale:
Elvis Presley's death certificate personally autographed by the president himself. Genuine. $5 each or two for $11.

*   *   *

"Thaddeus, why you make faces at the goldfish?"

"Well, he started it."

* * *

AT A DETROIT DANCE HALL

Berzlicki: Could you play "In The Mood?"

Bandleader: We just played it.

Berzlicki: I wish I'd known. It be my favorite tune.

* * *

Ziwacki couldn't stand it any longer, and so he went to the doctor to get treatment for his piles. He was given some suppositories and told to take two each day.

The following week, the Pole went back to see the physician. "How do you feel?" asked the medic.

"I be worse since I be taking these things. I had a hell of a time swallowing them."

* * *

POLISH PARTY RIDDLE

Ask for a volunteer from the group. Then give him these instructions. Place your right hand on your forehead as though you are trying to see a long distance. Place your left hand with your fingers cupped around the back of your head and ask, "What's this?"

* * *

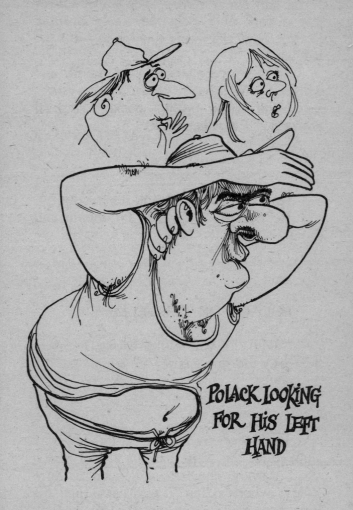

POLACK LOOKING FOR HIS LEFT HAND

Ryszard met a nice girl at a Polish social hall dance. Later, they wandered off into a park and spent the whole evening petting. Now they were running to catch the last bus.

"Put your fingers in your mouth and whistle to the driver!" suggested the girl.

"Not for a million bucks," replied Ryszard. "I'd rather walk!"

* * *

How does a Polack call for his dog?

He puts his fingers in his mouth and shouts, "Rover."

* * *

POLACK ON THE TELEPHONE

"Well, if you're the wrong number, then why did you answer the telephone?"

* * *

Every evening after work, Putsidwakim stopped in the same bar for a beer. Each time, Barney, the bartender, said to him, "Hey, where's Ben?" And each time the Pole answered, "Ben who?" The barkeep then said, "Bend over and kiss my rear!"

After weeks of this abuse, Putsidwakim

went to the bar across the street. He sat there grumbling to himself until Harry, the bartender, asked him what was wrong. The Pole told him what the other bartender said and how much it upset him.

Harry told him the next time he went back to Barney's place to ask Barney, "Hey, where's Eileen?" The bartender would answer, "Eileen who?" Then the Pole should say, "I lean over, and you kiss my rear!"

Putsidwakim thought this was a terrific idea. He walked across the street into the bar and shouted to the bartender, "Hey, where's Eileen?" The bartender said, "Oh, she ran off with Ben."

And the Polack said, "Ben who?"

* * *

Did you hear about the Polack who tied a knot in his pajamas to remind himself where his bedroom was and then ruptured himself trying to struggle into the legs?

* * *

WARSAW TV ANCHORMAN

"The Polish space program has run into technical difficulty. The astronaut keeps falling off the kite."

* * *

A pot of gold sat out in the middle of an intersection. On one corner stood Santa Claus; on another corner, the Tooth Fairy; on another corner, a smart Polack; and on the fourth corner, a dumb Polack. Who got the pot of gold first?

The dumb Polack because there is no such thing as Santa Claus, the Tooth Fairy, or a smart Polack.

* * *

What is considered a big night in a Polish neighborhood?

Watching the overloaded machines break down in the local laundromat.

Girlskis

What do a football player and a Polish girl have in common?

They both shower after the fourth period.

* * *

Why do Polish women wear high-heeled shoes?

To keep their knuckles from dragging on the ground.

* * *

"All right, Mrs. Zocronski," said the bill collector, "how about the next installment on that couch?"

"Okay," said the Polish woman. "I guess it's better than having to give you money."

*   *   *

Did you hear about the Polack who sold her typewriter because it missed two periods and she thought it was pregnant?

And then there was the Polish stenographer who wanted to goof off, so she called in dead.

*   *   *

Miss Koshuta entered the International Polish Beauty Contest and received a very strong recommendation. The judges recommended she go home and stay there.

*   *   *

"Can you make a martini?" the restaurant owner asked the Polish barmaid.

"No," she answered, "I don't put out for wops."

*   *   *

"How's Miss Poplawski, the new typist, working out?"

"Just great. She answers the phone every time her typewriter bell rings."

* * *

Miss Custak spent her summer vacation in Keansburg, New Jersey. When she got back to the office, she reported to Carmen, another stenographer.

"You'd never believe what happened to me on the beach."

"I'm listening," said the Puerto Rican girl.

"I went for a swim in my bikini. After diving under a wave, I found that the top of my suit was missing."

"That's terrible!" said Carmen. "What'd you do?"

"I did what any decent girl would do," said the Polish girl. "I covered my face with my hands and ran back to the hotel as fast as I could!"

* * *

A gynecologist was examining Sophie, a secretary. He told her to spread her legs, and peering in, he asked, "Have you ever had a checkup there?"

"I don't think so," said the Polish girl, "but I've had a few Rumanians."

A Polish girl was snapped on the beach at Lake Erie wearing a see-through bra—over her eyes.

* * *

Hopkins sat down in a Manhattan bar and after having a couple of drinks called the bartender over and said, "Give me another Scotch, and I wanna buy a drink for that Polish douche bag at the end of the bar."

"Hey," said the barkeep, "watch your language. We don't talk about our lady customers that way."

"All I said was I wanna buy a drink for that Polish douche bag."

"There you said it again—now don't do it!" warned the bartender.

"All right," said Hopkins, "I wanna buy a drink for that broad."

The bartender walked over to the woman and said, "The guy at the end of the bar wants to buy you a drink. What would you like?"

"Gimme a vinegar and water," she replied.

* * *

Have you heard about the Polish girl who came second in the beauty contest?
She was the only entrant.

And what about the Polish girl who has to take off her sweater to count to two?

* * *

Wiktoria came home and said to her father, "Papa, I'm pregnant."
He said, "Are you sure it's yours?"

* * *

A Polish woman arrived at the desk of a New York hotel and signed the registration card with an "O."
"Why did you put down that circle?" asked the clerk.
"I not able to write."
"Then why didn't you sign an 'X'?"
"I used be sign it that way," said the Polish woman, "but when I got my divorce, I took back my maiden name!"

* * *

Did you hear about the Polish girl who stood in front of the mirror with her eyes closed to find out what she looks like when she is asleep?

Then there was the Polish girl who thought kites were made from fly paper.

* * *

Bob Rosenfeld, California's brightest insurance broker, breaks up buddies with this cutie:

Miss Pilzudski was named as the "other woman" in a divorce case. In court, the lawyer began to question.

"Miss Pilzudski," he said, "Do you admit that you went to a motel with this man?"

"Yeah, but I couldn't help it."

"Couldn't help it? Why not?"

"He deceived me."

"How did he do that?"

"Well," said the Polish girl, "he told the clerk at the reception desk that I was his wife."

A DROBLIK DITTY

She Was Only a Polish Plumber's Daughter, But Every Time a Sailor Whistled, Her Cheeks Flushed

* * *

How can Polish parents tell if their daughter is old enough to own a razor?

They stand the girl in the middle of a room and make her stretch her arms straight out.

If the hair from under her arms reaches the floor, she's ready to start shaving it.

* * *

Two little Polish girls were walking down the street. One said to the other, "Do you know that I found a contraceptive on our patio the other day?"

The other girl replied, "What's a patio?"

* * *

Regina: I sending this letter to my boyfriend to tell him that the engagement be off.

Lillian: But the page is completely blank.

Regina: I know—but we not talking to each other.

The bank in the Cleveland suburbs had just opened. Miss Slovak walked in carrying a shopping bag filled with nickels, dimes, and quarters. "Did you hoard all this money by yourself?" inquired the teller.

"No," said the girl, "my sister whored half of it!"

* * *

Polish woman to taxi driver: "Could you back up sixty cents worth? I'm a little short of cash."

* * *

Mrs. Goldfarb was not too happy with the way Wanda, the new housekeeper, was cleaning the rooms. "There's so much dust on my dresser," she said, "I could write my name in it."

"Lady," said the Polish girl, "there be nothin' like education."

* * *

How do you get a Polish woman to burn her face?

Telephone her while she's ironing.

* * *

While cleaning the Clinton home, Krystyna the housemaid broke the penis of an ancient Greek statue. Quickly, she found some glue and put the marble male organ back in place, but in an erect position.

Later, Mrs. Clinton discovered the damage.

"Krystyna," she bellowed, "how could you do such a thing?"

"But, lady," said the Polish maid, "all them things I ever saw looked like that."

* * *

Did you hear about the Polish girl who was so thin she had the word FRONT tattooed on her chest.

There's a Polish girl whose mouth is so big when she smiles she gets lipstick on her ears.

* * *

"What are Miss Poland's vital statistics?"

"36-22-36."

"That's great."

"Yeah. And the other leg's the same."

* * *

Did you hear about the Polish girl who was so fat, whenever she had her picture taken, she was charged group rates.

And what about the Polish girl who was so fat, she had the mumps for two weeks before anybody knew it.

* * *

Harper pulled up to a Connecticut roadside vegetable stand. "How much do you charge for your spuds?" he asked.

"Spuds?" asked Miss Dembrowski. "What they be?"

"They're potatoes," said the tourist.

"I sure glad I ask you!" said the Polish girl. "Last week, I turn away man who want know if I had any *nookie* for sale. I bet if I asked what he meant, I be sittin' right on top of some!"

* * *

"Why isn't there any prostitution in Poland?"

"Take a good look at Polish girls and you'll realize they can't even give it away."

* * *

Alan Hoffman, Manhattan's premier CPA, turned in this titanic tickler:

The late train from Washington to New York was not very crowded. Miss Zimbriski was sitting opposite an advertising exec on his way home. She looked terribly sad and very lonely.

The man read his magazines, and then after a while he said to her, "Miss, excuse me, but would you like to take a look at my *Cosmopolitan*?"

"Mista," said the Polish girl, "if you dare try, I'll scream blue murder!"

Miss Slabodki got on a crowded Cleveland bus. She stood near Rick, a polite young man, who thought of giving his seat to her. Rick looked up and said, "How far?"

"You got your nerve!" snapped the Polish girl. "Would I ask you how long?"

* * *

Why can't a Polish girl give good head?
She can't get her lips over the guys' ears.

* * *

Prescott had been having a hot and heavy affair with Alicia. When he found he had to go to Tokyo on business, he presented his love with a beautifully wrapped box and said, "Here's a present for you. But don't open it unless you really miss me."

Three weeks later, he telephoned from Japan. "Hi ya, babe. Did you have to use what was in the box?"

"Oh, yeah, honey," said the Polish girl. "Three days after you left, I got so horny I opened it. Thanks for the vibrator. The only thing is, the first time I used it I shattered my two front teeth!"

* * *

* * *

Polish Girl:	Can you give me change for this 50 dollar bill?
Bank Clerk:	This isn't a fifty-dollar bill, it's a soap coupon.
Polish Girl:	My God, I've been raped!

* * *

Jacobson, the garment manufacturer, hired Miss Czarobski, a new secretary. One night, he took her to dinner at a private dining room in a smart supper club. As they finished their meal, Jacobson smiled and said, "Well, that's that. Now how about a little demitasse?"

"You men are all alike," said the Polish girl. "Don't even give you a chance to have a cup of coffee."

* * *

LUBLIN LOVE SONG

She Was Only a Polish Garbage Man's Daughter, But She Wasn't Anything To Be Sniffed At.

* * *

Miss Glazinski was enormously endowed. She had evidently gone to the Dolly
Parton School of Bust Development. One
night, she felt a little depressed and had a
few martinis. Later, the Polish girl left her
Baltimore apartment and wandered into a
cocktail lounge.

"Give me a martini!" she asked the
bartender.

When she'd finished that, she ordered
another. Then one more. Finally, she said,
"Give me another martini and take the pickle
out."

"It's not a pickle," said the bartender,
"it's an olive."

"Well, it's giving me heartburn," said
the Polish girl.

"It ain't the martini that's giving you
heartburn. You got one of your boobs in the
ashtray."

How can you spot fashion-conscious Polish girls?

They wear split-sided tights and stiletto-heeled bowling shoes.

* * *

Did you hear about the Polish girl who had her face lifted so it would be level with her nose.

Then there was the Polish girl who went to the dentist to have a wisdom tooth put in.

* * *

In a Detroit department store, a woman said to a clerk, "Can I boil this wool sweater?"

"Yeah," said the Polish salesgirl, "but only boil it in warm water."

* * *

BUFFALO BALLAD

She Was Only a Polish Lumberman's Daughter, But She'd Been Through The Mill

* * *

Mrs. Jablonski's son was ill in Ft. Wayne, so she went to the Western Union office to send him a telegram. When she got to the counter, she discovered that she had left her glasses at home. The kindly clerk offered to write out the message for her.

"No, I couldn't let you do that," said the Polish woman. "My poor boy wouldn't recognize your handwriting."

*   *   *

Did you hear about the Polish girl who was so thin she could stand on a bag of potato chips without crushing any.

And then there was the Polish girl who, if it wasn't for her Adam's apple, wouldn't have any figure at all.

*   *   *

"Oh, this suntan oil is useless," said Miss Szulecki, the secretary.

"How come?" asked Maria, a co-worker.

"I've drunk a dozen bottles of the stuff, and I'm still pale as a sheet," said the Polish girl.

*   *   *

One summer, Vince spent an entire Saturday sunbathing in the nude on the roof of his New York apartment building. The poor guy's whole body was burned almost to a crisp.

Later that night, while in bed with his Polish date, Vince was in agony. He tiptoed into the kitchen, poured a tall glass of cold milk, and submerged the object of his greatest discomfort.

"Oh, my God!" gasped the Polish girl, watching him from the doorway. "I've always wondered how men load that thing!"

* * *

Tricia and Daisy, two Polish waitresses, decided to live it up one Saturday afternoon. They went to see *Deep Throat*. The girls were seated in the back row of the theater watching the porno when suddenly Tricia leaned over and whispered to her friend, "The guy sitting next to me is masturbating!"

"Gosh," said Daisy, "tell him to stop!"

"I can't," said the Polish girl. "He's using my hand!"

* * *

Josie and Lida, two Polish high school seniors, met in the school cafeteria.

"Tell me all about the party you went to last night," begged Josie.

"It was great," said Lida. "Everybody drank two six packs of beer, and then they turned out the lights, and I got laid twice."

"Twice?" squealed Josie.

"Yeah, twice," said Lida. "Once by the football team and once by the basketball team!"

* * *

Miss Gurzeda, a pretty Polish model, nervously asked the doctor to perform an unusual operation—the removal of a large chunk of green wax from her navel. The M.D. looked up from the unusual mold and asked, "How did this happen?"

"You see, doc," said the Polish girl, "my boyfriend likes to eat by candlelight."

* * *

Magda, the little daughter of a Polish Seattle couple approached her mother and asked, "Mama, do people go to heaven feet first?"

"No, why you ask?"

" 'Cause yesterday Aunt Elizabeth was lying on the bed with her feet up hollering, 'Oh, God, I'm coming!' And she would have, too, if poppa hadn't held her down."

* * *

Miss Wenicki wandered into a clinic and said to the nurse, "I'd like to get a vassilation!"

"Excuse me," said the nurse, "I think you are talking about a vaccination."

"Yeah," said the Polish girl, "and I don't want you to give it to me on my arm 'cause I wear a sleepless nightgown."

"You mean sleeveless nightgown."

"And I don't want it on my thigh 'cause I have a zucchini bathing suit."

"You mean a bikini."

"And I don't want you to vaccinate me on my Virginia."

"You mean vagina."

"All right!" shouted the girl. "Virginia, vagina, just as long as I don't get small cox!"

* * *

Miss Kropski stood at the squad car and complained to the policemen. "This guy came up to my apartment with me," she said, "threw me on the bed, pulled off all my clothes, and then ran off with my purse!"

"Did you scream?" asked the officer.

"Of course not," said the Polish girl. "How did I know he was going to rob me!"

* * *

Miss Subzxyk said good night to her date with a long, lingering, wet kiss and shut her apartment door. The poor guy was so aroused he broke down the door, grabbed the girl, threw her to the floor, and began pumping away.

Ten minutes later, it was all over. "You really enjoyed that, didn't you?" he said. "I could tell 'cause your toes are all curled up!"

"Of course they're curled!" said the Polish girl. "I've still got my panty hose on!"

Churchskis

How can you tell when a Polack is getting ready to go to church?

He puts on a clean bowling shirt.

* * *

One of the cardinals was chosen to approach the new pope with a question. "Your Holiness," he said, "since you are so liberal, can we now go out with the nuns?"

"Yes," replied the pontiff, "as long as you don't get in the habit."

* * *

The new pope telephoned Begin and Sadat and congratulated them for winning the Nobel Peace Prize. Then he said, "I'm so pleased that the two of you could get together and settle your differences like good Christians."

Did you hear about the Polish optician who made Father Kaczka a new set of spectacles with stained-glass lenses?

* * *

Why did the new pope call himself Pope John Paul II?

The stationery was already printed and all he had to do was add a I to it.

* * *

Wiznecki walked into work sporting two black eyes. "What happened to you?" asked the foremen.

"I be in church yesterday. You know, I be good Catholic. Well, a big fat woman kneeling down in front of me have dress caught way up in crotch. So I pulled it out, and she punched me!"

"That accounts for one black eye," said the foreman. "How'd you get the other one?"

"Well, I could see she didn't like that," said the Polack, "so I shoved it back up!"

* * *

Hilde Sweeney, Santa Rosa's ebullient bookseller, gets belly boffs with this beaut:

The pope was being interviewed by an

American television reporter. "Your Holiness," said the correspondent, "you project such an aura of love. Everything you do or say is motivated out of love. You are such a loving man. Is there anything that you hate?"

"Yes," said the pope. "I hate Polish jokes, and I hate M & M's."

"I can understand why you can't tolerate Polish jokes," sympathized the reporter. "They portray Poles as being stupid. But why do you hate M & M's."

"Because," answered the pope. "I can never get the covers off."

* * *

Kozlowski and Czubek were sitting in a Toledo park having a smoke. "The pope has really got those Italians on their toes."

"How's that?"

"He raised the urinals at the Vatican six inches."

"Say, Kozlowski, what be a urinal?"
"How do I know—I no be Italian."

* * *

Did you know that the pope is collecting bowling balls to make a rosary for the Statue of Liberty?

* * *

What prayer does the pope say each morning with a big smile on his face?
, "Hail mary, full of grace,
The Wops are now in second place."

* * *

Why did the pope spend a million dollars on a degreaser?
He wanted to clean the throne.

* * *

Did you hear about the pope's latest decree?
Wafers of kielbasa will now be used for Communion.

* * *

What were the pope's words at his first papal blessing in St. Peter's square?
"All of you dagos off the lawn. I'm putting in flamingos."

* * *

Originally, the pope was going to call himself John Paul III, but the cardinals convinced him that two came before three.

* * *

At first, he didn't want the job of pope. He just didn't like the idea of living in an Italian neighborhood.

* * *

The pope's first act was to bless the cardinals.

Then the Giants, the Eagles, and the Jets.

* * *

The pope's first miracles:
He made a lame child blind.
He cured a ham.
He turned wine into water.

* * *

Why does the pope have TGIF embroidered on his red slippers?

Toes Go In First.

* * *

$$\begin{matrix} & 1 & \\ 3 & & 4 \\ & 2 & \end{matrix}$$

POPE'S FIRST LESSON

* * *

* * *

Did you hear the pope wants to wallpaper the Sistine Chapel?

* * *

One of the cardinals approached the pope and said, "Your Holiness, what do you think of the abortion bill?"
"Pay it."

* * *

"Your Holiness," asked a reporter, "how do you feel about priests marrying?"
"Only if they love each other."

* * *

Did you hear the new name of the College of Cardinals?
The College of Flamingos.

* * *

Did you hear they're replacing the organs in church?
They're going to use accordions.

* * *

How do you tell a cardinal from the pope?

The pope has "Captain" on his bowling shirt.

* * *

The pope was told by a gypsy fortuneteller that he must have a woman. "But that's impossible," replied the pontiff. "It is not allowed in our religion."

"That may be so," said the gypsy, "but if you do not have a woman, you will lose everything. You will be forced to leave the Vatican, you will no longer be pope, your whole world will come crashing down."

The pope explained this meeting with the fortuneteller to his first cardinal and asked, "What shall I do?"

"You must do as the gypsy says. I will get you a woman."

"All right," agreed the pontiff, "but only under three conditions. First, she must be blind. In that way, she will never be able to see who she is sleeping with.

"Second, she must be deaf and dumb. In that way, she'll never be able to tell what happened.

"And third, she's gotta have nice big boobs!"

* * *

Why are they building a tavern behind the Vatican?

So the pope will have a place to cash his paycheck.

* * *

PAPAL PROCLAMATION

Priests will no longer wear vestments —from now on they are to wear bowling shirts.

* * *

"Has the pope stayed a nice, down-to-earth, old-fashioned Pole?"

"He certainly has. When His Holiness gives his blessing, he turns around and on the back of his robe, it says: VATICAN LANES."

* * *

Father Adamska made young Jozef promise to stop his excessive masturbation.

"Save it for when you get married, my boy," said the padre.

"Okay, I'll do it," said the youngster.

Two weeks later, Father Adamska met the boy and asked how he was doing.

"Good," said the young Polack, "so far I've saved about a pint and a half."

* * *

VATICAN NEWS RELEASE

"The pope has decided to make Good Friday—Tuesday."

* * *

It was his wedding night, and Minister Zybryski finished brushing his teeth in the bathroom. He came out and found his bride lying naked on her back in bed. The clergyman was shocked.

"I expected to find you on your knees."

"Okay," said the Polish girl, "but it always gives me the hiccups!"

* * *

Zdzislaw sat before the doctor and asked, "Is masturbation harmful?"

"The current attitude," replied the M.D., "is that it depends on the frequency."

"Three times a day, that be too much?"

"Of course. Why don't you get yourself a girl?"

"I got me girl."

"No," said the doctor. "I mean one who understands."

"She understand real good."

"Then why do you have to masturbate three times a day?"

"She be religious," said the Polack. "She don't like it during meals."

Miss Kalicki sat in the confessional. "Father, I've truly sinned," said the girl.

"How my child?" asked the priest.

"I met this stevedore yesterday afternoon, and last night he took me out and hugged me and squeezed me and kissed me all night and made love to me eight times."

"Go home," said the priest. "Go home and squeeze the juice out of six lemons and drink it down."

"Oh, father," said the Polish girl, "will that serve as my pennance?"

"No, but it'll wipe the smile off your face."

Wlodzimierz joined the army and after a few months decided to write home.

"I'm stuck on something," he said to the chaplain. "Is there a hyphen in hard on?"

"Huh?" gasped the clergyman, "whatever are you telling your folks in that letter?"

"Not much," answered the Polish soldier. "I'm telling mom and dad we're finally able to attend services in your field chapel—the one we worked so hard on."

* * *

An Ohio firm wanted to promote some shop workers, and Wilson, the manager, a deeply religious man, interviewed candidates for the better-paid jobs. Wilson thought a knowledge of the Bible qualified a man as much as his skill at work. When Grimaldi entered, he asked him, "Who were the earthly parents of Jesus?"

"Eh, Joseph and Mary," said the Italian.

"Good," said the manager, and then proceeded with the more technical side of the interview.

Grimaldi finished the interview and then told his friend Stadnicki, "Wilson asked me who the parents of Jesus were. I told him Joseph and Mary."

"Holy smoke," said Stadnicki, "I never remember that."

"I'll write it on your cigarette pack," said Grimaldi, "so you can hide it in your hand."

Stadnicki stood before the manager, his cigarette package on which was written in block letters "Joseph and Mary" concealed in his big palm.

"Ah," said Wilson, "name two of Jesus Christ's disciples."

The Polack stared down at the cigarette pack and said, "Er, Benson & Hedges?"

Brideskis and Groomskis

Modjeska was getting married and asked the druggist for a jar of Vaseline. Next day, he walked in and said, "Hey, this Vaseline ain't no use—you better give me some alum."

* * *

"I just came from a Polish wedding."
"How was it?"
"Different. The bride was so ugly that everyone kissed the groom."

* * *

How can you tell when there's a Polish wedding?
The first and third garbage trucks have their lights on.

* * *

Mrs. Szulecki had been married only three days. She walked into a drugstore and asked for a bottle of men's deodorant.

"The ball type?" asked the clerk?

"No," she replied, "for under his arms."

* * *

Did you hear about the Polack whose wife wanted a coat made of animal skin?

He gave her a donkey jacket.

And what about the Polack who cut off his dong because it got in his way when he made love?

* * *

Janicki the farm boy had been making love to a hole in a tree. Unfortunately, there was a hornet's nest in the tree trunk, and the hornets stung his penis. Later, on his wedding night, he took a heavy stick and thrust it into his bride's vagina, grinding it in all directions like a pestle.

"What the hell you doing?" she screamed.

"Don't worry," said the Polack. "If there be any hornets' nest in this hole, this is one time I ain't getting caught!"

* * *

* * *

Stash and Eva got married and went on their honeymoon. The clerk at the hotel said, "The bridal suite is all ready!"

Stash said, "That's fine for the bride. What about my room?"

* * *

Mrs. Karpuik: I went to Niagara Falls for my honeymoon, and I had a terrific time.

Mrs. Renatti: How did your husband enjoy the falls?

Mrs. Karpuik: Oh? You supposed to take your husband along, too?

* * *

Rudzilski came home one evening and found his new bride in a sad mood. "I was pressing your suit," she explained, "and I burned a big hole in the pants."

"Don't worry," said Rudzilski. "I got an extra pair of pants for that suit."

"Oh, I know," said the Polish woman. "I cut a piece out of them to patch up the hole."

* * *

Zaleski and his new bride checked into a suburban Chicago motel. The groom climbed under the covers and said, "Will I be the first to do this to you?"

"What a dumb question!" said the Polish girl. "I don't even know what position ya gonna use yet!"

* * *

After Ethel and Zeke had a lovely Polish church wedding, Zeke said, "Let's be good Americans and have a black baby."

"Okay," said the new bride.

Nine months later, Ethel gave birth, and the baby was white. Their second baby was white. A year later, she gave birth to another white baby.

"We must be doing something wrong." said Zeke. "I ask Willie where I work."

Zeke cornered the huge black foreman and asked him why they couldn't have a black baby.

"Hey, man, has you got a dong that's fifteen inches long?"

"No," answered Zeke.

"Is your dong five inches wide?"

"No," replied Zeke.

"Dat's your answer," said the black man.

"You's lettin' in too much light."

Have you heard about the Polish woman who was ironing her husband's socks?
She burned his feet.

Then there was the thoughtful Polack's wife who served her husband baked beans with pineapple juice because she liked Hawaiian music.

* * *

Two Polish teenagers came home from their honeymoon. The next day, the bridegroom found his wife crying in the kitchen.
"What's the matter, honey?" he inquired.
"I rinsed the ice cubes in this hot water, and now I can't find them." she exclaimed.

* * *

Did you hear about Mrs. Kowalchek's bowl of wax fruit?
It went rotten.

And what about the Polish housewifc who thinks a can opener is the key to the john?

* * *

It was a lovely summer morning. The sun was shining, and the sky was a bright blue without a cloud to be seen. All eyes were turned toward Mrs. Glowicki, who was walking down the street with her huge left breast exposed. A man stopped her with a somewhat embarrassed look and pointed it out.

"Oh, my God!" cried the Polish woman. "I left my baby on the bus!"

* * *

"Hey, why are you cutting that block of ice into little cubes?"

"So they'll fit into the ice tray," said the new Polish housewife.

* * *

Mrs. Corrigan was newly married and in the process of redecorating her husband's house. She noticed a hand print on the bedroom wall that had been freshly painted the day before. Dressed in a flimsy negligee, Mrs. Corrigan stood at the head of the stairs and called down to Karpinski, who was painting the living room.

"Excuse me," she said, "but would you like to come up here and see where my husband put his hand last night?"

"I like to, lady," said the Polack, "but I got to get done with this painting first."

* * *

"This meat don't taste too good," said Michalak to his wife.

"I can't imagine why," she replied, "I burnt it a little, but I put sunburn oil on it at once."

* * *

POLISH HOUSEHOLD HINT

In hot weather, put a bucket of manure in the center of the dining table to keep the flies off the food.

* * *

Janusz wanted to marry Juanita, a Mexican girl, but her parents forbade it. The unhappy couple decided to jump off the tallest building in Los Angeles.

Only the girl hit the ground. The Polack got lost on the way down.

* * *

"Hey, this meringue tastes funny."

"Well, I made it according to the recipe," said Mrs. Kosek. "It said to separate two eggs, so I left one egg on the kitchen table and the other one on the window ledge."

* * *

Szymon's wife turned to him at breakfast and said, "Take that tie off. It clashes with the curtains."

* * * .

"Say," groaned Zygmount, "I thought we gonna have spaghetti for dinner."

"So did I," said his wife, "but my saucepan ain't long enough."

* * *

Old Piotrowski and his wife were visiting New York and decided to eat at an expensive restaurant. They each ordered a big four-course dinner with steak as the main course. When the meal was served, the Polack began eating immediately, while his wife sat looking at her plate for over ten minutes.

"Isn't the meal to madam's satisfaction?" asked the head waiter.

"Sure," said the Polish woman, "but I be waiting for husband to finish with the teeth."

* * *

Did you hear about the Polish housewife who had an accident while ironing the curtains?

She fell out of the window.

Then there's the Polack who never sleeps with his wife.

He claims she's a married woman.

* * *

Kozcynski's new bride came home with a clear-plastic mini-dress and held it up for her husband's approval.

"Say," exclaimed Kozcynski, "you can see right through it."

"No you can't, dummy," said Mrs. Kozcynski. "Not when I'm in it."

* * *

The salesman stood at the front door of the Markowski house.

"I don't want a vacuum cleaner," exclaimed Mrs. Markowski, "I don't have any vacuums to clean!"

* * *

Have you heard about the Polack who decided to have only three children?

He heard that one in every four children born is a Chinese.

* * *

And what about the newly married Polish girl who wanted her husband to take One A Day vitamins but couldn't figure out the dosage?

* * *

Chet Wander, America's master bridge guru, gets guffaws with this goofy gag:

Korzcynski and his wife were celebrating their twenty-fifth wedding anniversary. As a surprise, he walked into the house with a little monkey.

"Hey, what be that?" asked Mrs. Korzcynski.

"It be a monkey. What the hell does it look like?"

"But what you bring him here for?"

"That be wedding present for you," said the Pole.

"You crazy!" she exclaimed. "What we gonna do with a monkey?"

"He gonna eat with us, he gonna sleep with us . . ."

"Sleep with us!" shouted the wife. "What about the smell?"

"Listen," said the Polack, "after twenty-five year, if I could get used to it, so will the monkey."

Wiznecki was suspicious of his wife. One day, he left work early, went home, and found a strange hat and umbrella in the hallway. His wife was on the couch in the living room astride another man. Wild for revenge, the Pole picked up the man's umbrella and snapped it in two across his knees.

"There!" shouted the Polack. "Now I hope it rains!"

* * *

During a Las Vegas trip, Haskins, a wealthy home builder, fell in love with a pretty Polish chorus girl. Two weeks later, they were married. After the honeymoon, Haskins gave a big dinner party at his country estate for friends. While he went to the cellar to choose some special wine, the guests were chatting in the living room.

When Haskins returned, he found everyone heading out the door. "Why is everyone leaving?" he asked his new bride.

"I don't know," said the Polish girl. "They were talking about rats in their houses, and someone said the best way to get rid of them was to pound broken glass in their holes. And I said, 'But how do you get the rats to hold still long enough?' "

* * *

The Zareckis were having a battle royal.

"That's the second clean shirt you've had on this month," screamed his suspicious wife. "Have you got a broad on the side?"

* * *

Zubelwicz screamed at his wife, "The bank just returned this check for one hundred dollars!"

"That's great," said Mrs. Zubelwicz. "What should I buy with it this time?"

* * *

Mrs. Wishnak told her lawyer she wanted a divorce. "On what grounds?" he asked.

"My husband has be unfaithful," she said.

"What makes you think so?" the lawyer asked.

"Well," said the woman, "I not think he be the father of my child."

* * *

Leon: Can't we keep our marriage a secret?
Dora: But suppose we have a baby?
Leon: Oh, we'll tell the baby, of course.

* * *

Matt Kowalski, the popular Palm Beach retiree, loves this playful pearl:

Rostenkowski, a Bronx steel worker, was in a bitter mood. He stomped into the kitchen one morning and shouted at his wife, "Hey woman, why are my work socks full of holes?"

"Because, stupid," answered Mrs. Rostenkowski, "you asked me to boil them. And I had to keep prodding them with a fork to see if they were done."

"I had a beauty today at the adoption center," said the volunteer to her husband.

"What do you mean?"

"A Polish couple adopted a three-month-old war orphan and decided to learn Vietnamese so they'd understand what the baby was saying when it grew up."

* * *

Kowalski was quite worried about his wife, and so he went to see a psychiatrist about her. "She's got this terrible fear of having her clothes stolen" he said.

"How can you tell?" asked the doctor.

"Only the other day I got home early and found that she hired a man to stay in the closet to guard them."

* * *

"You're not gonna believe this, Ryan."

"What's that, Rafferty?"

"My neighbor Rutkowski, the Polack, just castrated himself."

"What?"

"Yeah. He's real jealous of his wife, and he says now if she gets pregnant, he'll know positively she's been cheatin' on him."

* * *

In the maternity hospital waiting room, Piludski shouted, "I'm a father, I'm a father! Have a cigar."

"Thanks. Is it a boy or a girl?"

"I don't know. All cigars look alike to me."

* * *

The Osbornes hailed from Kansas City and were motoring through Michigan. When they reached Hamtramck, an argument ensued as to the correct pronunciation. The husband insisted on pronouncing the second m—the wife equally was sure that she was correct. "There's only one way to settle this," said Mr. Osborne. "We'll ask a native. Let's stop here for lunch."

The waiter was Polish. "Would you mind slowly pronouncing the name of this place?" asked the husband.

"Okay," said the Polack. "D-A-I-R-Y Q-U-E-E-N."

* * *

Luigi greeted Bogaslaw at the corner saloon. "Hey," said the Italian, "you best friend is up at you apartment right now boffing you wife."

"What?" screamed Bogaslaw as he flew out the door. "I kill that dirty bum!"

In ten minutes, the Polack returned to the bar. "Hey," he said to the Italian, "you made me run up a whole flight of stairs for nothing. Telling me my best friend be making love to my wife. I never saw *that* guy before in my life."

* * *

Wojawicz and Kozlowski were driving home from work. "Let's stop and get a beer at this great new place I found," suggested Wojawicz. "The bar stools are numbered and if your number is called, you can go upstairs and get free sex."

"No kidding?" said Kozlowski. "Did you ever win?"

"No," said Wojawicz, "but last week my wife won twice!"

* * *

Funnyman Joe Bingo tells about Korczak and his buddy Lopez, who were having a beer after work. "No kidding," said the Mexican. "You say you meet your wife in a whorehouse. That's really somethin'!"

"Nah, it be embarrassing," said the Polack. "I thought she be home minding the kids, and she thought I be bowling. And on top of that, the madame refused to refund my money or give me another girl.''

* * *

Manzini picked up a sexy-looking blonde at a Long Island bar and took off in his car. They parked in a dark alley and *made it* in the back seat three times. Before she could ask for more, the Italian said, ''Baby, I gotta get a pack a cigarettes. I'll be right back!''

Down the street, he ran into Lobada, his drinking buddy. ''Pal, I got a regular nympho in the back seat of my car,'' said Manzini. ''All you gotta do is to get in and boff her. It's all the same to this broad. She'll take on anybody.''

Lobada found the car, opened the back door, groped around in the dark for the girl, and immediately the two of them were locked in embrace.

In a few moments, a flashlight beam struck them in the face. ''What're you two doing in there?'' asked the cop.

''It's all right, officer,'' offered the Pole. ''This lady is my wife!''

''Oh, I'm sorry,'' said the cop. ''I didn't know!''

''Neither did I,'' said the Polack, ''until you shined the flashlight in the car!''

Propkowicz died, and his widow went to the funeral parlor to make the burial arrangements.

"Everything you ask will be done, Mrs. Propkowicz," said the mortician. "But there is something I don't understand."

"What that?"

"Why do you want your husband buried face down with only his bare behind sticking up out of the ground?"

"Oh," said Mrs. Propkowicz, "that be so when I come to visit grave, I have some place to park my bicycle!"

Famous Peopleskis

Many legendary Poles have made extraordinary contributions to America and its culture. Gen. Casimir Pulaski was a hero in the Revolutionary War. So was Thaddeus Kosciusko, who helped defeat the British in 1777. Leopold Stokowski and Artur Rubenstein are names that will live forever in musical history. But what about the lesser-known greats? Everyday folks who have done the unusual, the remarkable. Here are some exceptional Poles whose unconventional deeds and accomplishments you've never heard about:

The Polish scientist who developed an artificial appendix.

* * *

The Polish secret agent who wrote all his messages in invisible Braille.

123

The Polish major who resigned after he received a letter marked private.

* * *

The Polish widow who wears black garters in remembrance of those who have passed beyond.

* * *

The Polish spy who committed suicide by slipping arsenic in his coffee while looking the other way.

* * *

The Polish motorist who, every ten thousand miles, changed the air in his tires.

* * *

The Polish crook who turned himself in hoping to get a reward.

* * *

The Polish girl who opened the cellar window to let out the darkness.

* * *

The Polish astronomer who got fired because he wouldn't work nights.

* * *

The Polish professor who crossed a Jersey cow with a masochist and got cream that whips itself.

* * *

The Polish housewife who thought you could tell the age of an onion by counting the rings.

* * *

The Polish girl who spent two weeks in a revolving door looking for a doorknob.

* * *

The Polish plastic surgeon who specialized in repairing Tupperware.

* * *

The Polish farmer who crossed bees with lightning bugs, and now he has bees that can work at night.

* * *

POLISH MERCEDES

MORE POLES YOU'VE NEVER HEARD OF

The Polish ventriloquist whose dummy quit to find a new partner.

* * *

The Polish eunuch who entered himself for the No Ball Prize.

* * *

The Polish girl whose appendix was taken out more times than she was.

* * *

The Polack who bought a pet rock? The next day it ran away.

* * *

The Polish godfather.
He'll make you an offer you can't understand.

* * *

The Polish mosquito.
It died of malaria.

* * *

The Polish poultry rancher who crossed a turkey with a centipede so everybody could have a drumstick.

*   *   *

The Polack who stuck his head in the oven because he wanted a baked bean.

*   *   *

The Polack who tried to grow a handle-bar mustache but it kept falling off the front of his bike.

*   *   *

The deaf Polack who had a habit of talking to himself. He looked in the mirror so he could read his lips.

*   *   *

The Polack who took his new tie back to the shop because it was too tight for him.

*   *   *

The Polish digital watch.
It only goes up to ten. After that, you have to take off your shoes.

*   *   *

The Polish carpenter who was stranded on a desert island for two years.

One day, an empty lifeboat floated up to his island, so he broke it up into bits and made himself a raft.

* * *

The Polish pansy who stuck his tongue out at the bartender and told him to put a head on it.

* * *

The Polish hooker who was so ugly she ended up working in a doghouse.

* * *

The Polish farmer who ran a steamroller across his fields because he wanted to market mashed potatoes.

* * *

The Polish streetwalker who was so exclusive she had an unlisted telephone booth.

* * *

The Polish athlete at the Olympics who won a gold medal and went out and had it bronzed.

* * *

The Polish plumber who looked at Niagara Falls and said, "Give me time and I could fix it!"

* * *

The Polish street cleaner who went beserk following a merry-go-round.

* * *

The Polish woman running after a garbage truck this morning yelling, "Taxi, taxi!"

* * *

The Polish saloon keeper who created a beer glass with a magnifying bottom for watching television.

* * *

A Pole who came up with a variation on the traditional Swiss cuckoo clock that is a big seller in Polish neighborhoods: the bird comes out and farts the time.

AND SOME MORE POLES YOU SHOULD KNOW ABOUT

The Polish starlet who was interviewed by so many producers she was too tired to do the screen test.

* * *

The Polish immigrant who ran off the bus backward because he heard a woman passenger say she was going to pinch his seat when he got off.

* * *

The Polish teenager who explained to his doctor that he contracted VD during a wet dream.

* * *

The Polish bride of a GI who wrote to the army for her husband's favorite food recipes.

* * *

Nine to Fiveskis

Szymcyk applied for a teaching job at Yale and was asked questions on Greek mythology. "Which creature was half man and half beast?"

"Would that be Buffalo Bill?" said the Polack.

* * *

Lopanecki got a job working in a storeroom. His first assignment was to put THIS END UP labels on a couple of hundred crates.

A little later, when asked if he had managed to do it, he answered, "Yeah, and in case they couldn't be seen on the top, I put them on the bottom, too."

* * *

Have you heard about the Polack who got a job as quality control officer in a banana factory?

They had to sack him because he kept throwing away all the ones that were crooked.

Then there was the Polack who invested all his savings in frozen radio dinners.

* * *

The well-meaning social worker told unemployed Runicki, "I think you'd find a job much faster if you took a bath and changed your shirt once in a while."

"Hey," said the Polack, "why look for trouble?"

* * *

Ski was looking not too hard for a job.

"I can get you a job digging potatoes," offered the unemployment counselor.

"Why don't you get the man that planted them?" asked Ski. "He knows where he hid them."

* * *

Santucci was hired to wash the windows of an 18-story building. When he arrived at the job, he discovered Fudzynski and Luczak were there to help him. The Italian and the two Poles climbed on a scaffold and pulled themselves up to the top floor. An hour passed, when suddenly Santucci climbed over the scaffold and leaped eighteen stories to the street below. He died immediately.

The police arrived, and one of the officers asked Fudzynski and Luczak, "How'd this happen?"

"I don't know," replied Luczak. "Maybe it be because of his deformity."

"What do you mean?"

"Well," explained the Polack, "he kept saying that he couldn't work with two assholes."

* * *

Kraczyski was standing on a ladder painting the ceiling. Halicki came into the room and asked, ''Got a good hold on that brush?''

''Yeah,'' said Kraczyski. ''Why?''

''Hang on tight. I be moving the ladder into the next room.''

* * *

It was dead winter, and Danecki was sitting in a Minneapolis employment office.

''I can offer you a job driving a snow plough,'' said the owner.

''What, in this weather?''

* * *

Why was the recent Polish H-bomb test such a total failure?

Somebody forgot to bring along a match to light the fuse.

* * *

Lee Bonnett, the Wyoming railroad honcho, says, ''In Poland, an institution of higher learning is any grade school with a second floor.''

* * *

Why do Polacks find it so hard to read?
Because they have never learned to move their lips properly.

* * *

Did you hear about the two Polacks who went into the loan shark business?
They lent out all their money and then skipped town.

Then there was the Polish bank robber who wanted to be fashionable, so he wore a see-through ski mask.

* * *

Wlassak got a job with the highway department painting the stripe down the middle of Route 101. The first day, the Polack reported painting five miles. Mr. Bales, his supervisor, was really happy with him.

The second day, Wlassak reported painting only three miles. Bales figured the Pole just had an off day.

The third day Wlassak reported painting only one mile. "How come you keep decreasing your work output?" asked the supervisor.

"The reason be," said the Polack, "it be further back to the paint can each time."

* * *

How can you tell the Polish gardener?
He's the one watering the garden during the rainstorm.

How can you tell the intelligent Polish gardener?
He's the one holding an umbrella while watering the garden during a rainstorm.

An old Dodge pickup truck pulled up in front of a Chicago lumber yard. Koszyczki left his partner, Bezublik, sitting in the cab and approached the foreman. "I want some three by four's," he announced.

"We only got two by four's," said the lumber man.

"Wait, I got ask Bezublik."

Koszyczki returned and said, "Okay."

"How long do you want them?" asked the foreman.

"I check with my partner."

Koszyczki came back in a minute and said, "We want them for a while—we building a house!"

*   *   *

Did you hear about the Polish farmer who gave his sheep iron pills so that he would get steel wool?

Or the Polack who turned down a blow job because he was afraid they would stop his unemployment insurance?

*   *   *

Grabowski got a job in the post office for the Christmas rush. He was assigned the sorting of letters, and he got good at it. In just one day, the Pole had become the fastest letter sorter in post office history.

The postmaster was quite pleased and said, "Son, you are the fastest letter sorter I have ever seen. You could have a great future with the post office if you are interested?"

"Thank you, mista," said the Polack. "Tomorrow I do even better. I try to read the addresses."

* * *

Ziolkowski got a job as a plumber. It was his first day on the job. When the phone rang, he picked up, and the caller said, "I got a leak in my bathtub."

"Go 'head," said the Polack. "It won't hurt nothin'."

* * *

Neighbor: What with inflation, the cost of living is so high I'm gonna raise my own chickens this year.

Bolicki: Me, too. See these eggs? I gonna plant them today.

* * *

Did you hear about the Polack who was filling out an application for employment?

In the blank printed CHURCH PREFERENCE, he wrote: *Red Brick*.

* * *

Alan Bresee, the Hollywood video technical genius, gets giggles with this nifty nonsense:

Bolewicz and Potacki, two furniture movers, spent thirty minutes wrestling with a heavy dresser that was wedged on a landing.

"It no good," said Bolewicz. "We never gonna get it upstairs."

"Upstairs," said Potacki. "I thought we were trying to get it downstairs."

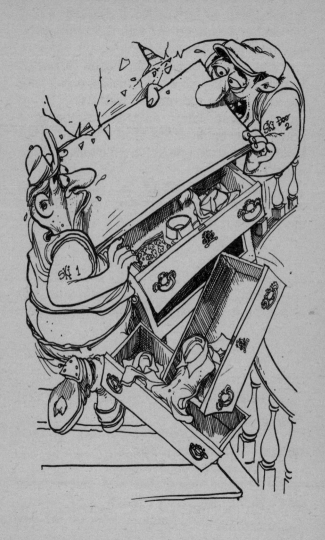

The people of New York City were up in arms, and so Mayor Koch decided to act. He declared war on the rats threatening the health of New Yorkers.

His Honor ordered the health inspector to send nine Polish exterminators down into the sewers to wipe out the rodents.

A month later, only six of the nine Poles came back. "For God's sake," cried Koch, "what happened to the other three men?"

"They defected to the enemy," announced the inspector. "And out of the six that returned, two brought back war brides."

* * *

Then there was the Polack who put iodine on his paycheck because he got a cut in pay.

* * *

Dielecki moved to North Dakota and applied for a job.

"Have you any experience in coal mining?" asked the clerk.

"Yeah, in Pennsylvania."

"They're using that new safety lamp down there now, aren't they?"

"I not know, mista. I work on the day shift."

*   *   *

Lomanicki came to work at eleven o'clock one morning, and his boss shouted, "You should have been here two hours ago."

"Why?" asked the Polack. "What happened then?"

*   *   *

Did you hear about the Polish postman who looked everywhere for a round mail box so he could deliver a circular letter?

Then there was the Polish secondhand car dealer who turned back all the fuel gauges.

*   *   *

Polucki went for a job on a building site.

"You'll have to pass a test question," said the foreman. "Can you tell your left hand from your right?"

"Sure," said the Pole.

And the foreman rubbed his hands together, remarking, "It's a cold morning."

"Play fair now," said the Polack, "don't shuffle them."

*   *   *

"Why are you late for work, Kozlicki?"

"Well, sir, when I looked in the mirror this mornin' and couldn't see myself, I thought I'd gone to work. Two hours later, I found the glass had fallen out."

* * *

Balducci rushed into a hardware shop and shouted, "Give me a mousetrap, quick. I've got to catch a bus!"

"Sorry," retorted Garbinski, the sales assistant, "but our traps won't catch anything bigger than a rat."

* * *

NEWS ITEM

Polish gravediggers have gone on strike but will still handle emergencies.

* * *

Did you hear about the Polack who applied for a job as a deckhand on a submarine?

Or the Polack who was so honest he worked in a Turkish bath for three years and never took a bath?

* * *

Boleslaw met his friend Kosek at the supermarket.

"I just been offered a job as precision engineer," said Boleslaw. "Only trouble be, I got be able to measure things in thousandths of an inch."

"My God," said Kosek, "how many thousandths are there in an inch?"

"I don't know but there must be millions."

* * *

Super Studley, the top Tinsel Town photographer, gets snickers with this knee slapper:

Wazalewski ran into his friend Roszka. The two men had migrated from Poland together.

"Where you working now?" asked Wazalewski.

"In a steel mill," he replied, "although I was on a farm before that."

"Why you leave there?"

"The food be real bad. An old sheep die there one day, and we had eat mutton for days. Then an old sow died, and we ate bacon and pork for weeks. But when the old woman die a month later, I pack my bags right away!"

* * *

Milt Larsen, the California variety arts theater impressario, gets roars with this wacky wisp of whimsy:

A Polish jet liner was winging its way toward John F. Kennedy Airport in New York. As it approached, the pilot established radio contact.

"Hello, tower, this be Wojie Yablonka, aboard Flight 621 from Warsaw."

"Hello, Flight 621," answered the air traffic controller. "What is your height and position?"

"I be five feet nine inches tall, and I be in the front of the plane!"

Dumbrowski and Kubiak went into an employment office looking for work.

"What do you do?" the assistant asked Dumbrowski.

"I be a pilot," he answered.

"Good, we need pilots," came the reply. "And what do you do?"

"I be a woodcutter," said Kubiak.

"I'm afraid we don't need woodcutters."

"Wait a minute," asked Kobiak "how can my friend pile it if I don't cut it?"

* * *

At the union hall, the leader stood up and spoke to the members: "First, the bad news. We had to settle for five percent reduction in wages. Now the good news. We managed to get it back-dated six months."

* * *

Motorist: Did you fill my car with gasoline?

Janowski: Yeah, I did, mista, but when I opened the door, it all ran out!

* * *

Did you hear about the Polish forger?

The FBI broke into his house and took away half a million nine-dollar bills.

Then there was the depressed Polack who decided to kill himself with an overdose of aspirin.

But after taking the first two, he felt much better.

* * *

Foreman: Okay, you got the job. Now how much do you want a week?

Zywicki: Three hundred dollar.

Foreman: Three hundred dollars! But you're unskilled.

Zywicki: Yeah, but the job always be much harder when you not know anything about it.

* * *

Fiedosiuk was taking the examination for the sanitation department and was not doing too well. For his final question, he was asked, "What does *tempus fugit* mean?"

"It mean," said the Polack, "I don't get no job."

* * *

What job do Polacks request most down at the unemployment office?

Scuba diver for Roto-Rooter.

* * *

Wojewodzki became tired of city life and convinced his wife they should move way out in the country. The Pole purchased a chicken ranch but soon discovered that all his chickens were laying sterile eggs.

At a loss to what was causing it, Wojewodzki decided on a plan of action. He went to town and bought himself a shotgun. Returning to the ranch, he hurried into the hen house, pushed the rooster up against the wall, and said, "Okay, mista cock, where you be hiding the condoms?"

"This saw won't cut a thing."

"That's funny. It was all right when I sawed a brick with it yesterday."

* * *

Jancywicz the house painter was discussing a job with a Grand Rapids home owner.

"What will you charge me to paint my house?" asked the man.

"Fifty dollar a day" replied Jancywicz.

"You're kidding!" exclaimed the home owner. "I wouldn't pay Michelangelo that price!"

"Listen, mista," said the Polack, "if that wop be doing job for less, he no be member of the union!"

* * *

Leokowarda, a construction worker, had been constipated for a month, so he went to Dr. Schwartz. The M.D. examined his backside and suggested he get it unblocked with a pneumatic drill.

"What good would that do?" asked the Polack.

"It would break up the concrete that's attached to your back passage," said the physician. "And another thing. From now on, when you go to the toilet, don't wipe yourself with a discarded cement bag."

Did you hear about the Polack who opened up a laundromat business right beside a church because a friend told him that cleanliness is next to godliness?

Then there was the Polish postman who resigned because he said the new postal codes were too difficult to pronounce.

* * *

Halicki and Goldberg each managed a general store directly across the street from each other. Customers constantly came out Goldberg's store, all carrying two or more purchases. But business was bad for the Polack's store.

Finally, Halicki consulted his competitor.

"How come you do so much business?" he asked.

"Suggestive selling," explained the Jewish manager. "For example, when I sell a woman grass seed, I also sell her a lawnmower."

Later that day, a woman walked into Halicki's and bought a box of sanitary pads. The Pole suggested that she buy a lawnmower, also.

"Now why in the world would I need a lawnmower?" asked the customer.

"Well, you ain't able to make love," replied the Polack, "so you might as well mow the grass."

Inventskis

The world is familiar with the discoveries made by universally recognized Poles such as Copernicus (astronomy) and Madame Curie (medicine). Perhaps not so commonly known is the birth of the bagel. The "roll with the hole" was created in 1883 in honor of King John Sobiesky and introduced in America by Harry Lender, an immigrant from Lublin, Poland, in the twenties. However, there are numerous other creations that the public is not aware of. Here are just a few of many original Polish inventions:

Dietetic Ex-Lax

* * *

Garlic-flavored Listerine

* * *

Carbonated toilet water

*　*　*

Waterproof sponge

*　*　*

Wisdom dentures

*　*　*

Filter-tip chewing gum

*　*　*

Inflammable poker

*　*　*

A paper paperweight

*　*　*

Open-toed bowling shoes

*　*　*

An iron-on deodorant

*　*　*

Indelible skywriting

* * *

Parfum de bowling shoes

* * *

An I-fart-your-weight machine

* * *

Four-poster sleeping bag

* * *

Electric chair-seat warmer

* * *

A snot bank

* * *

Topless bulletproof vest

* * *

Thermal sun hat

* * *

An ear trombone

* * *

Roll-on tear gas

A one-armed bandit for the disabled

* * *

Lighthouse moat

* * *

A home for unmarried babies

* * *

A shit-powered fan

* * *

Rocking chair sickness pills

* * *

Inflatable sledgehammer

* * *

Cast-iron pin cushion

* * *

Flounder-flavored douche

* * *

Chocolate-covered Vaseline

College Examskis

PART ONE

1. Who won the Second World War?
   Who was second?
2. What is a silver dollar made of?
3. Write down your name. (Candidates are advised not to copy.)
4. Spell the following: dog—cat—fish.
5. What time is *News at Eleven* on?
6. Approximately how many commandments was Moses given? (State whether you just guessed.)
7. Write down the numbers 1–10. (Marks will be deducted for every number out of sequence.)
8. Who is buried in Grant's tomb?
9. What color is a red fire engine?
10. Write down all you know in not less than three words.

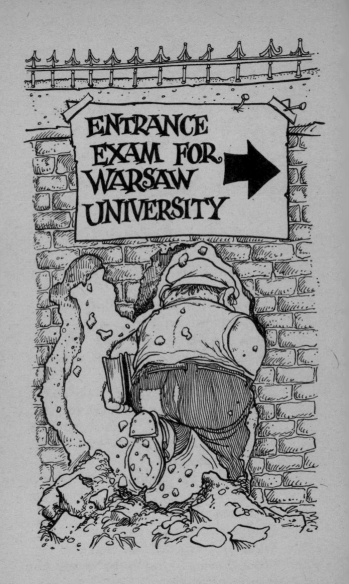

PART TWO: COUNT YOUR NOSE

How many noses do you have? Can you find out? Count your nose with your finger and write your answer below.

How many noses you have: 1_____ 2_____ 3_____.

ANSWER: One

WORD HUNT

There are four words hidden in this word puzzle. Can you find them?

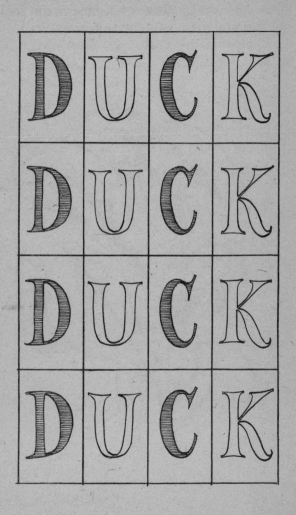

FIND THE AARDVARK IN THE BACK
OF THE PICKUP TRUCK

There is an Aardvark hiding in the back of this pickup truck. Can you find him?

CONNECT THE DOTS

○
 1

○
 2

WORD SEARCH

Find the word in the word list by look-ing across, down, diagonally, forward or backward. Circle the word you find.

WORD LIST

Cat

GET THROUGH THE MAZE

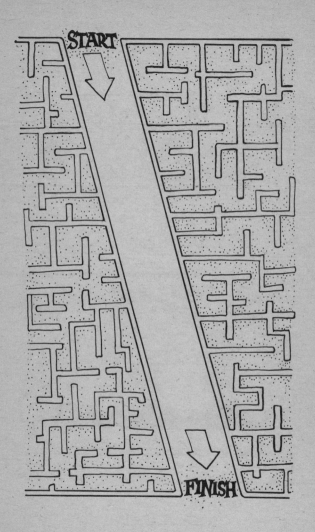

DIFFERENT?

Tell which object is different. Try your skill.

Can you find the hidden elephant in this picture?

Vocabulary test: Write answer beside each.

1. │ SAND │ = SAND BOX

2. MAN   MAN
   ─────
   BOARD = OVERBOARD

3. STAND =
     I

4. R/E/A/D/I/N/G

5 WEAR
  LONG

6. CYCLE
   CYCLE
   CYCLE

7. LE VEL

8. T
   O
   W
   N

9. 0
   ─────
   M.D.
   Ph.D:
   M.B.A.

10.
$$\frac{I \qquad I}{O \qquad O}$$

11.
$$\frac{MIND}{MATTER}$$

12.
$$\frac{GROUND}{\begin{array}{c}FEET\\FEET\\FEET\\FEET\\FEET\\FEET\end{array}}$$

13. DICE   DICE

14. DEATH   LIFE

15. PUNISHMENT

16. HE'S   HIMSELF

17.
CHAIR

18.
TOUCH

19.
```
  R
ROADS
  A
  D
  S
```

20. ECNALG

(ANSWERS ON NEXT PAGE)

ANSWERS TO PART THREE

1. | SAND | = SAND BOX

2. $\dfrac{\text{MAN}}{\text{BOARD}}$ = MAN OVER BOARD

3. $\dfrac{\text{STAND}}{\text{I}}$ = I UNDERSTAND

4. R/E/A/D/I/N/G
   READING BETWEEN
   THE LINES

5. $\dfrac{\text{WEAR}}{\text{LONG}}$ = LONG UNDERWEAR

6. CYCLE   TRICYCLE
   CYCLE
   CYCLE

7. LE VEL   SPLIT LEVEL

8. T   DOWN TOWN
   O
   W
   N

9. $\dfrac{0}{\text{M.D.}}$
   M.D.   3 DEGREES
   Ph.D.   BELOW ZERO
   M.B.A.

10. $\dfrac{\text{I} \quad \text{I}}{\text{O} \quad \text{O}}$ CIRCLES UNDER THE EYES

11.   <u>MIND</u>   MIND OVER
     MATTER   MATTER

12. <u>GROUND</u>
    FEET   6 FEET
    FEET   UNDER GROUND
    FEET
    FEET
    FEET
    FEET

13. DICE DICE   PARADISE

14. DEATH LIFE   LIFE AFTER
                    DEATH

15. PUNISHMENT   CAPITAL
                 PUNISHMENT

16. HE'S HIMSELF   HE'S BY
                 HIMSELF

   CHAIR
17.   HIGH CHAIR

18.   TOUCH DOWN
   TOUCH

   R
19. ROADS   CROSSROADS
   A
   D
   S

20. ECNALG   A BACKWARD
               GLANCE

Odds and Endskis

Why is the wheelbarrow the greatest of all human inventions?

It taught the Polacks to walk on their hind legs.

* * *

How do you recognize a Polack in a carwash?

He'll be sitting on his bicycle.

* * *

Mrs. Chernak received a sternly worded notice from her bank that her checking account was overdrawn.

Embarrassed, Mrs. Chernak sat right down, wrote a note of apology, and sent them a check.

Did you hear about the Polish mosquito? It bit Dolly Parton on the arm.

Then there was the Polack who laid a Chinese girl and an hour later he was horny again.

* * *

In the woods of northern Michigan, a Polish raccoon and a regular raccoon were caught in traps. "Hey," said the regular raccoon, "just chew off your leg like I just did and you can escape."

Three weeks later, he returned and found the Polish raccoon still in the trap. "I told you to chew off your leg and you'd get out of the trap."

"You be nuts!" exclaimed the Polish raccoon. "I chewed off three legs already, and I still be caught in the trap."

* * *

Korsak and Rizzuti met in prison when they were given the same cell. "How long you in for?" asked Korsak.

"Eight years," replied the Italian.

"Oh," said the Polack, "you better take the bed by the door. I'm in for ten, so you'll be leaving before me."

* * *

Krezslaw lived in a remote mountain village. One morning, he was awakened by the postman delivering a letter.

"You shouldn't have come all that way just to bring me one letter," said the Polack. "You should've mailed it."

*   *   *

Partyka told Gonzales, a drinking buddy, "I just read about experiments showing that the tar and nicotine in cigarettes cause cancer in rats and mice."

"What you gonna do about it?" asked the Mexican.

"I outsmarted them." said the Polack. "I put all my cigarettes on the top shelf where the rats and mice can't get at them."

*   *   *

Why do Polacks make the best secret agents?

Even under torture they can't remember what they have been assigned to do.

*   *   *

How many Polacks does it take to carry out a kidnapping?

Ten. One to capture the kid and nine to write the ransom note.

* * *

Le Beau, Shapiro, and Dolistowski were sentenced to thirty years in prison. Each was given one request that would be honored by the warden.

"A woman," asked the Frenchman.

"A telephone," said the Jew.

"A cigarette," said the Polack.

Thirty years passed, and the three were let out of jail. The Frenchman walked out with ten kids. Shapiro strolled out carrying a $10,000 commission he had made during the time.

The Polack walked out and said, "Hey, anybody got a match?"

* * *

"I finally gave up smoking," said Drakich.

"Why's that?" asked a coworker.

"I just got fed up. I was using three matches every time I wanted to get a flame from my cigarette lighter."

* * *

Did you hear about the counterfeit ring that was broken up in Hamtramck?

The Polacks were making $2 bills by erasing the zeros off of $20 bills.

Then there was the Polack who cut off his arms so he could wear a sleeveless sweater.

* * *

"Ma," said young Zbigniew, "why are all the women in Detroit always so tired?"

"Why you ask such a question?"

" 'Cause every place we go, I see a place marked 'Ladies' Rest Room'."

* * *

A rule in a Polish nudist camp is that members must wear a colored tape around their wrists to distinguish the men from the women.

* * *

Did you hear about the Polack who cut off his fingers so he could write shorthand?

Or the Polack who cut off his hands so he could play the piano by ear?

Or the Polack who cut off his left leg and left arm so he could be all right?

* * *

Lucinda Dyer, the pretty book publicist, pleases pals with this dandy:

Halicki was standing at the rail of the Staten Island ferry boat watching the waves. A young woman stood near him. Suddenly, the girl's hat blew off in the wind, and when she tried to grab it, she fell overboard.

As she splashed around in the water, she shouted up, "For God's sake, drop me a line!"

"Okay," shouted back the Polack. "What's the address?"

Berzlicki walked up to a policeman.

"Have you seen a crazy man?" he asked.

"What does he look like?" asked the patrolman.

"He be short," said Berzlicki. "Only six feet four, and he very thin. He weigh about four hundred pound."

"If he's short, how could he be six feet four, and if he's very thin, how could he be four hundred pounds?"

"I told you he be crazy," answered the Polack.

* * *

Young Ski: Ma, will you buy me an encyclopedia?

Mother: No, you walk to school like the rest of the children.

* * *

A small town in Poland decided to build a bridge, and the council was debating its construction.

"Which side of the river," asked the councilman Cyrankiewicz "has the most traffic?"

"The south side," answered the clerk.

"Good," said the councilman. "Then that will be the side we must build the bridge on."

182

Terry Radtkey, the consummate California carpenter, roars over this cackler:

Giovanni and Konarski were talking.

"Where'd you go on your vacation?" asked the Italian.

"A nudist colony," answered Kornarski.

"No kiddin'? What's it like?"

"Terrible," replied the Polack. "I never felt so embarrassed walkin' around with my money in my mouth."

* * *

How many Polacks does it take to wash a car?

Two. One to hold the sponge and one to drive the car back and forth.

* * *

Grzegorz was the best chauffeur in Chicago as well as an expert mechanic.

The wealthy society matron who employed him had only one complaint: He was extremely sloppy about his own appearance.

One day, she decided to lecture him on his weakness.

"Grzegorz," she began, "how often would you say it is necessary to shave?"

"With a weak growth like yours, ma'am," replied the Polack, "I think every third day would be enough."

Ladislas decided to write to the *Guinness Book of Records* and claim that he should be included. He explained that at one time he had been the youngest person in the world.

* * *

Did you hear about the Polish bank clerk who spent all his spare time sitting in a tree.

He wanted to be a branch manager!

* * *

O'Rourke and Bolinkowicz were walking along when the Irishman took a breath of air and shouted, "Wow, did you crap in your pants?"

"No," replied the Polack.

"Are you sure?" questioned O'Rourke.

"Yeah," said Bolinkowicz.

"Are you lying?" asked the Irishman.

"No," answered the Polack.

"I'd better see for myself!" said O'Rourke, pulling down the Polack's pants.

"Y-e-e-c-ch! They're covered with crap. I thought you said you didn't crap in your pants," exclaimed the Irishman.

"Oh," said the Polack, "I thought you meant today."

How can you tell if a Polack is an aristocrat?

His tattoo has no spelling mistakes in it.

* * *

Husarski joined the army and after three years' service was awarded the special crossed knife and fork insignia. This was to celebrate three years of eating with a knife and fork without accident.

* * *

Then there was the Polack whose sister had a baby. Nobody told him if it was a boy or a girl, so he didn't know if he was an uncle or an aunt.

* * *

Dabrowski rushed into Giordano's shoe repair shop and shouted at the owner, "You dumb wop!"

"Wattsa matta wid you?" asked the Italian.

"I told you to make one shoe bigger than the other, and instead of that you made one smaller than the other."

* * *

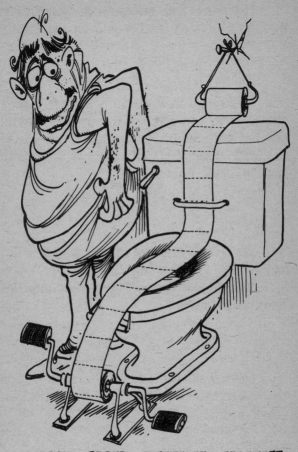

POLISH PAPER RECYCLING MACHINE
PATENT # 623

Did you hear about the Polack who locked his keys in his car?

He waited two hours for the Auto Club to arrive to open the car and let his family out.

Then there was the Polack who sent a check for $100 to his aunt as a birthday gift, but he didn't sign it because he didn't want her to know who sent it.

* * *

Why don't Polacks eat pickles?
They can't get their heads in the jar.

* * *

Waluk was sitting at a bar with his buddy, Bongavani.

"What does a polar bear do?" asked Waluk.

"I don't know," answered the Italian. "I guess he sits on ice."

"Sits on ice?" asked the Polack.

"Yeah, there's nothing else to sit on."

"What else does he do?"

"He eats fish," said Bongavani.

"Sits on ice and eats fish. Then I not gonna accept."

"What ain't you gonna accept?"

"I won't accept," said the Polack. "I was invited to be a polar bear at a funeral."

*   *   *

While on vacation in California, Siwicki visited the Los Angeles zoo and wound up standing in front of the kangaroo cage for hours.

The keeper noticed him and asked, "What's so fascinating?"

Siwicki pointed at the sign that read *A Native of Australia* and said proudly, "My sister married one."

*   *   *

Fran Legum, the pretty Washington schoolmarm, tells about old Mrs. Duffy, who was going on vacation. The Irish woman asked Resnicki, her neighbor, to look after her goldfish. When she returned, Mrs. Duffy asked him if he had changed the water.

"Of course not," replied the Polack. "They didn't drink what I gave them last week."

*   *   *

How can you tell a Polish airplane in a snowstorm?

It's the one with the chains on the propellers.

*   *   *

You can always tell the Polack on an oil rig on the North Sea.

He's the one throwing bread to the helicopters.

* * *

Chernik and Kazewski went hunting in upstate New York. They took along two guns and three dogs. Half an hour later, they came back for more dogs.

* * *

Mrs. Jablecki called up the fire department and shouted, "There's a fire! There's a fire!"

"How do we get there?" asked the fireman.

"What happened to your big red truck?"

* * *

Have you heard about the Polack who lost $100 on the Kentucky Derby?

Then he lost $150 on the replay.

Then there was the Polack who made a fortune by taking up a collection for the widow of the Unknown Soldier.

* * *

*　*　*

In a small community near Lublin, Polecki and Slowacki each had a horse, but they had great difficulty in telling them apart. So Polecki cut off his horses's tail. Everything was fine, but then Slowacki's horse had an accident and unfortunately lost his tail. Now the two men found themselves right back where they started. The Polacks decided to consult Dr. Dodrecki, the famous university professor, to see if he could help them.

He looked at the two horses for a while and then said, "It's really quite easy. That bay mare is about half a hand bigger than that gray stallion."

*　*　*

Did you hear about the Polish dairy farmer who made all his cows sleep on their backs?

He wanted the cream to be on the top in the morning.

Then there was the Polack who lost his toupee in a cow pasture and tried on six before he found it.

*　*　*

NEWS BULLETIN

A Polish mountaineering expedition was unsuccessful in its assault on Everest. It ran out of scaffolding just a few feet short of the summit.

* * *

"What did the Polack answer when he was asked, 'How much is two times two?'"
"I don't know."
"That's right."

* * *

Kowalski went to a doctor for an examination. The M.D. put a tongue depressor in the Polack's mouth, looked down his throat, and said, "Kowalski, you've got flat feet."

"Hey, doc," said the Polack, "do me a favor. Look up my ass and see if my hat's on straight."

* * *

Why did the Polish helicopter crash?
It got chilly, so the pilot turned off the fan.

* * *

191

Paul Ryan, Hollywood's hospitable cable talk show host, gets howls with this hunk of high jinks:

Marciszewski, the great Polish detective, arrested a crime-hardened jailbird on the streets of Warsaw. He was about to handcuff him when a huge gust of wind blew the detective's hat off.

"You want me to go and get it?" asked the criminal.

"Do you take me for a fool?" said the Polack. "You wait here while I go and get it!"

Doreen: Close the car door!
Jefrem: But I wanna make love with the lights on.

*   *   *

Chalecki and Fascza were riding in an old pickup truck down a dusty Ohio road. Suddenly, the vehicle picked up speed going down a steep hill. "My goodness," shouted Chalecki, "the brakes don't work!"

"Don't worry," said Fascza, "there be a stop sign down at the bottom."

*   *   *

Stash and Ski were walking along the street one afternoon when a man carrying a bowling ball approached them. Stash grabbed the man's bowling ball and sent it crashing to the ground. The ball broke into pieces.

"Hey," said Ski, "why you do that?"

"You kiddin?" asked the Polack, "that be one darkie that'll never hatch."

*   *   *

Did you know that the bagpipe was invented in Poland in 1235?

They were trying to make an accordion.

*   *   *

The morning after a bitter Buffalo snowstorm, Brvdzena came out to the front of his house to see how deep the snow was. He noticed that the sidewalk of his neighbor, Panelli, was completely clear.

"How you get rid of all the snow?" asked Brvdzena.

"Easy," answered the Italian. "I started a fire and burned it all way."

"That be good idea," said the Polack, "but then what you do with all the ashes?"

*   *   *

Did you know that a lot of the Polacks were injured during the black riots in Detroit?

The Polacks were throwing dynamite sticks at the blacks. The blacks were catching them, lighting them, and then throwing them back.

*   *   *

Did you hear about the Polack who bought a stepladder and carefully put a sign on the top rung: STOP HERE.

Then there was the Polack who thought a wood screw was an orgy at a lumber yard.

*   *   *

195

* * *

PARLOR GAME

Hold your nose with one hand and flap the other arm. Ask: "What's this?"

(Answer) A vulture flying over a Polish picnic.

* * *

Dombrowski walked into a Pittsburgh sporting goods store and began trying on baseball caps. Thirty minutes later, he said to the clerks, "Hey, ain't you got one with a peak at the front?"

* * *

George Bernardi, the brilliant financial oracle, beams broadly over this bit of burlesque:

Rojek and Tarkian were seated next to each other at a bus station.

"Let's play a game of riddles," said Tarkian.

"Okay," said the Polack. "How you play?"

"It's easy," explained the Armenian. "You tell a riddle, and if I can't answer it, I'll give you five dollars—and vice versa."

"Well, I not so smart as you," said

Rojek. "So I think you ought to give me ten dollars if I can no answer."

"Okay," said Tarkian. "You go first."

"What have four legs, two of them in the air, and thirteen eyes?" asked the Pole.

Tarkian thought for a moment and then said, "I give up. What is it?"

"I don't know, either," said the Polack, "and here be your five dollars."

* * *

The Great Renaldo, Wisconsin's whimsical wizard, provided this rollicking rib ticker:

It was right in the middle of winter, and Hanna's father, Bozyslawa, trudged through the snow to her boyfriend's house. He complained to the boy's father, Kusielwicz, that his son went and urinated in Bozyslawa's back yard.

"You know how it is," said Kusielwicz. "Boys will be boys."

"Yeah," said Bozyslawa, "but he spells his name out in the snow."

"Okay," said Kusielwicz, "but why're you so upset?"

"You kiddin?" screamed Bozyslawa, "it be in my daughter's handwriting."

* * *

*   *   *

A Greek freighter sailing the South Pacific was hit by a fierce hurricane. Huge seas broke the ship apart, and it sank immediately. Only three seamen survived: Gorecki, Benzini, and La Touche. After drifting several days in a lifeboat, the Pole, Italian, and Frenchman washed up on an uncharted island.

Even though the island was deserted, there must have been inhabitants at one time, for there was a thatched hut, and the men found plenty of berries, fruit, and fish to live on. One day, several months later, a plane flew over. The men waved frantically, and when the pilot spotted them, he dropped a walkie-talkie by parachute.

Over the transmitter, they explained what had happened to them, and then the Frenchman said, "When will you rescue us?"

"Sorry," answered the pilot, "the weather is too bad this time of year to pick you up, but I'll come back once a week and drop you supplies."

From then on, each Tuesday there was a drop by chute: food, medical supplies, *Newsweek*, toilet paper. But after six months, the men were getting a little buggy. "Hey," said the Italian over the walkie-talkie one day, "why doncha drop us a woman."

"Maybe I can fix you guys up," returned the pilot.

The following week, the plane flew over and dropped a large package. The men unwrapped it and found an inflated rubberized woman. She was beautiful. "I'm first," exclaimed La Touche. The French sailor dragged her into the hut. Two hours later, he joined his buddies and said, *"Magnifique!"*

"Now it's my turn," announced the Italian. He rushed into the hut and spent the next three hours with the blown-up female. When Benzini finally staggered out of the hut, he was smiling from ear to ear.

"Okay," said Gorecki, "now I gonna have my chance."

In two minutes, he was back. "Hey," said the Italian, "why are you back so soon?"

"Mon dieu! What happened?" asked La Touche.

"You won't believe it," exclaimed the Polack. "I bit her tits, and she farted and flew out the window."

* * *

NEWS ITEM

Observe National Be Kind to Polacks Week February 30th to 37th.

* * *

199

What is a big awkward animal with a
trunk?

A Polack on vacation.

* * *

Andrzej and Barbara were driving
through the outskirts of Milwaukee.

Barbara: Can you drive with one hand?
Andrzej: (Excitedly) You betcha, honey
bunch.
Barbara: Well, wipe your nose. It's running.

* * *